THE HIDDEN VOICES SERIES

Bonds of Justice:
The Struggle for Oukasie

Kally Forrest

   HIDDEN VOICES

Published by Fanele, an imprint of Jacana Media (Pty) Ltd in 2019

10 Orange Street, Sunnyside
Auckland Park
Johannesburg 2092
South Africa
+27 11 628 3200
www.jacana.co.za

Text © Kally Forrest, 2019
Index © Karin Pampallis, 2019
Cover image © G. de Vlieg

All rights reserved.

ISBN 978-1-928232-84-1

Editing by Nkhensani Manabe
Proofreading by Linda Da Nova
Index by Karin Pampallis
ABC Press, Cape Town
Job no. 003530

See a complete list of Jacana titles at www.jacana.co.za

   HIDDEN VOICES

The financial assistance of the National Institute for the Humanities and Social Sciences (NIHSS) towards this publication is hereby acknowledged. Opinions expressed and conclusions arrived at are those of the author and editors and are not necessarily to be attributed to the NIHSS.

Bonds of Justice

Contents

Foreword...vii
Acknowledgements.................................. x
Maps..xii
Abbreviations xiv

ONE
Oukasie Fires Up: The Beginnings of Struggle............. 1

TWO
Oukasie Resists – "We Shall Not Be Moved!" 21

THREE
The Backlash 66

FOUR
The People's Municipality: Oukasie Development Trust..88

FIVE
A New Era and a Difficult Birth 112

SIX
Afterword 138

Notes 149
Bibliography 158
Index 162

Foreword

THE HIDDEN VOICES PROJECT emerged out of an interest in left intellectual contributions towards discussions on race, class, ethnicity and nationalism in South Africa. Specifically, the project seeks to examine and make available writings by hidden voices – voices outside of the university system or academic voices suppressed by apartheid pressures. Before and during the apartheid years, many universities were closed to existing local ideas and debates, and critical intellectual debates, ideas, texts, poetry and songs often originated outside academia during the period of the struggle for liberation.

The Hidden Voices Series seeks to publish key texts, books, documents and other materials that were never published under apartheid, or seminal books that have gone out of print. We hope that these recovered, lost or forgotten voices will help to reinvigorate the humanities and social sciences and contribute to the decolonisation of knowledge production in South Africa, and indeed throughout Africa.

This fourth volume in the Hidden Voices Series – *Bonds*

of Justice: The Struggle for Oukasie – is a new publication based on research carried out in Oukasie, a township in the Madibeng municipality, by Kally Forrest, a researcher at the Society, Work and Development Institute at the University of the Witwatersrand. Most of the interviews were done in 2011 and 2012, but a newly written afterword brings the book up to date. We applaud Dr Forrest for her outstanding work and keen insights.

Bonds of Justice: The Struggle for Oukasie tells the story of a dedicated group of young people who were members of the Young Christian Workers (YCW) and trade unions, as well as the Oukasie Development Trust and other local organisations. They were motivated by their belief that accountable and responsible leadership was needed to improve the situation of their community and its members. Together, they developed an "informed, reflective and strategic programme of participatory action to bring change" (Chapter 6, this volume). That approach succeeded in mobilising the Oukasie community. In the early 1980s they engaged in organising many workplaces in and around Brits and gaining better conditions for the workers there. Later in the 1980s they succeeded in stopping the apartheid government's attempt to forcibly remove Oukasie's residents. In the early 1990s they were successful in improving the living conditions of the community's residents by developing water and electricity services, roads and amenities such as a library and clinic. The book goes on to describe the problems faced by Oukasie and the wider community when the ethics of accountability were forgotten later in the 1990s and early 2000s.

The book has many lessons for South Africa today – not least among them the benefits that accountable governance can achieve, and what the costs are when a more selfish approach takes root.

This book, and indeed the entire series, has been made possible by the generous support of the National Institute for the Humanities and Social Sciences. The Institute was established in December 2013 to advance and coordinate scholarship, research and ethical practice in the field of humanities and the social sciences (HSS). Its catalytic projects aim to encourage research in new areas of engaged HSS scholarship.

Karin Pampallis and Edward Webster
Hidden Voices Project
Johannesburg, January 2019

Acknowledgements

IT WAS A PLEASURE researching this book. The people of Oukasie were generous with their information as together we revisited their startling and yet, for many, forgotten journey. A big thanks to those who spent long hours with me talking, discussing and piecing together this history. And to Jacob Moatshe, a special thanks for his ongoing availability to answer my questions.

Gratitude goes as well to others from outside Oukasie who shared important parts of its history, and who also gave generously of their memories. Thank you, too, to Madibeng Council which gave me open access to their Council minutes.

The unpublished "The History of Brits Old Loction, Oukasie" by T. Mangoathe, N. Matlhare, S. Shozi, M. Mongoathe and D. Mathebula gave me a number of insights including into how Oukasie activists evaded detention during the State of Emergency. Jean-Marie Dumortier's book, written in French, and translated for me by Drew Forrest – thanks, Drew! – conjured up the excitement and tension of key moments in Oukasie's history.

The book is filled with Gille de Vlieg's wonderful images, and Taffy Adler contributed the uplifting picture taken on the night of Oukasie's first electricity light-up – streets filled with light after a dark period in the community's history! Paul Weinberg's image gives a sense of workers' strong identification with their unions, while Bernie Fanaroff's photos of Joyce Modimoeng's funeral bring alive the tenacity and courage of Oukasie's residents.

Thank you to the reviewers who evaluated the manuscript of this book for the Hidden Voices Series, Alan Morris and Nicole Ulrich, for their useful comments. And a special thanks to the Hidden Voices Project, including Karin Pampallis, who was a thorough editor, ensuring the text was accessible to readers of all kinds, and to Edward Webster who has been continually supportive.

The research was done under the auspices of the Local Histories and Present Realities NRF/SARChI Chair at the University of the Witwatersrand. Its former head, Professor Philip Bonner, now deceased, supported me in writing this history and I am grateful for his encouragement and comments.

Kally Forrest

Maps

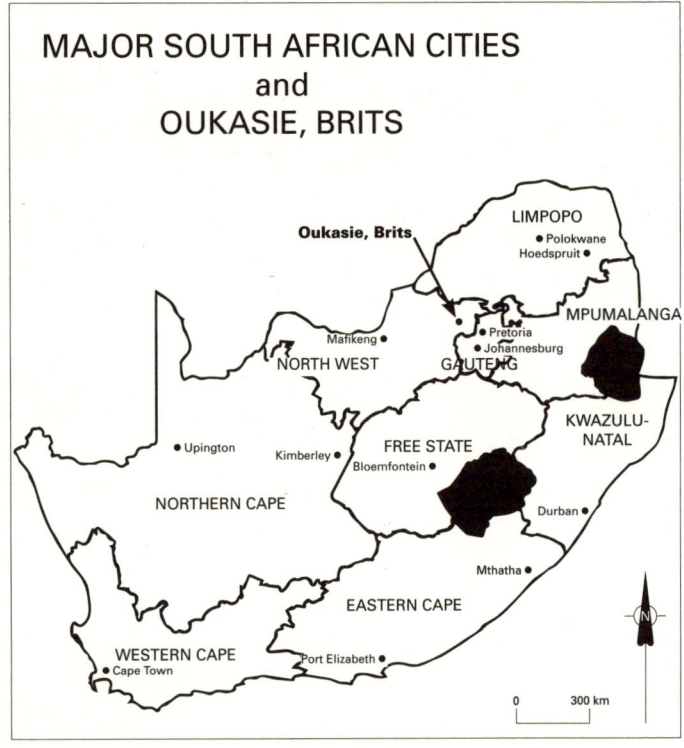

South Africa, showing post-1994 provincial boundaries

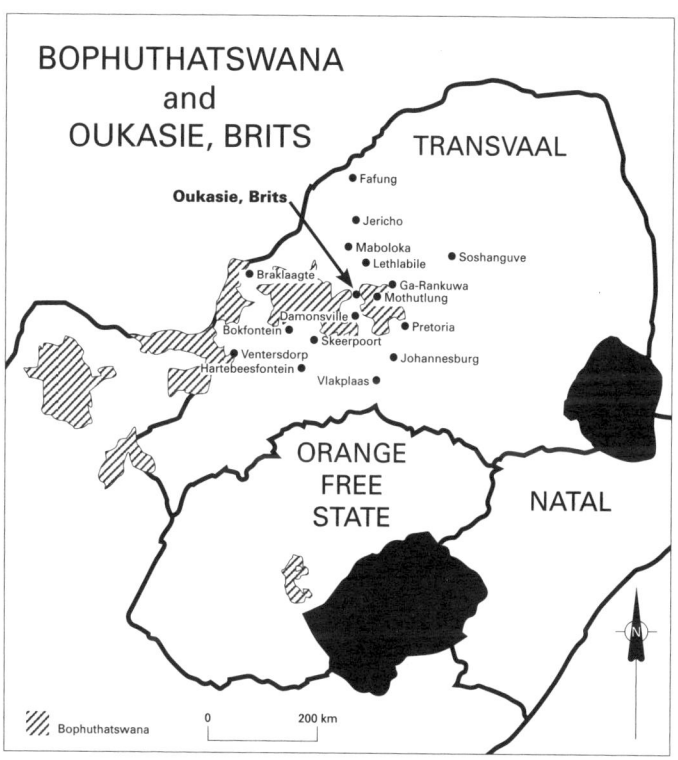

Pre-1994 map showing the position of Oukasie/Brits in relation to Bophuthatswana homeland borders. The Transvaal province roughly equated to present-day North West, Limpopo, Gauteng and Mpumalanga provinces.

Abbreviations

AAC	Alexandra Action Committee
ACDP	African Christian Democratic Party
ANC	African National Congress
AWB	Afrikaner Weerstandsbeweging
B&S	[steel manufacturing company in Brits]
BAC	Brits Action Committee
Bop	Bophuthatswana
CEO	Chief Executive Officer
COSAS	Congress of South African Students
COSATU	Congress of South African Trade Unions
CP	Conservative Party
DA	Democratic Alliance
DP	Democratic Party
FCI	Federated Chamber of Industry
Femco	[refrigeration factory in Brits]
FOSATU	Federation of South African Trade Unions
GBDF	Greater Brits Development Forum
GBIG	Greater Brits Investment Group
HNP	Herstigte Nasionale Party
HR	Human resources

IDP	Integrated Development Plan
IDT	Independent Development Trust
IEC	Independent Electoral Commission
LEBULLDTA	Lethlabile–Brits United Local and Long Distance Taxi Association
LRC	Legal Resources Centre
LTA	Lethlabile Taxi Association
MAWU	Metal and Allied Workers Union
MK	Umkhonto we Sizwe
NAAWU	National Automobile and Allied Workers' Union
NAFCOC	National African Federated Chamber of Commerce and Industry
NDR	National Democratic Revolution
NECC	National Education Coordinating Council
Nats	National Party or National Party members [also known as Nationalists]
NP	National Party
NPM	New Public Management [model]
NUM	National Union of Mineworkers
NUMSA	National Union of Metalworkers of South Africa
OCA	Oukasie Civic Association
ODT	Oukasie Development Trust
OWM	Oukasie Women's Movement
PFP	Progressive Federal Party
RDP	Reconstruction and Development Programme
SABC	South African Broadcasting Corporation
SACBC	South African Catholic Bishops Conference
SACC	South African Council of Churches

SACP	South African Communist Party
SACTU	South African Congress of Trade Unions
SAFTU	South African Federation of Trade Unions
SAMWU	South African Municipal Workers' Union
SANCO	South African National Civic Organisation
SANSCO	South African National Student Congress
SEIFSA	Steel and Engineering Industries Federation of South Africa
SEP	Science and Education Project
SEWUSA	Steel Engineering and Allied Workers' Union of South Africa
TLC	Transitional Local Council
TPA	Transvaal Provincial Authority
TRAC	Transvaal Rural Action Committee
TRC	Truth and Reconciliation Commission
TUCSA	Trade Union Council of South Africa
UDF	United Democratic Front
US	United States
YCW	Young Christian Workers
YCWSA	Young Christian Workers South Africa

ONE

Oukasie Fires Up: The Beginnings of Struggle

BRITS IS A TOWN about 60 kilometres north-west of Pretoria. Its main road still bears the name Hendrik Verwoerd Avenue as it passes through the town and leads on to the old location, Oukasie. This rutted thoroughfare carries memories of an ultra-conservative town, and still harbours a busy industrial centre that continues to operate despite neglected infrastructure. This small town was the site of remarkable struggles for freedom, dignity and justice. The black inhabitants of Oukasie took their fight to the seemingly invincible apartheid government. This book tells their nearly forgotten story.

Founding of Brits and Oukasie

The town's roots go deep into Afrikaner history. It was founded in 1924 on the Roode Kopjes farm and named after the owner, Johannes Nicolaas Brits, who came from Voortrekker stock. It was the scene of Afrikaner unity in the Transvaal in the 1860s when, following independence from Britain, skirmishing Boer groups signed an armistice treaty. A speech by General Hertzog in 1912 at the nearby De Wildt railway station led to the formation of the National Party (NP), and the town was the scene of a procession of horsemen during the 1949 country-wide pageant that was trekking to the Voortrekker Monument in Pretoria.[1] The Nazi-influenced Ossewabrandwag had strong support in Brits during World War II; a number of its members were imprisoned by the Union government, including future prime minister B.J. Vorster.[2] This conservative Afrikaner history was to weigh heavily on the black people of Oukasie in later years.

This book focuses on Oukasie's story. Oukasie originated as a transit labour camp in 1927 and had, until 2005, never been formally designated as a township. In consequence, no housing had been provided by the state since 1930. By the 1980s, however, its ramshackle self-built housing, lush surroundings, twisted alleyways and close bonds between people bore testimony to a firmly established community. The township hovers on the edge of the town of Brits and hides a rich seam of buried history. A group of now ageing but once young, energetic and innovative residents were a vital part of that history.

In 1968 the National Party demarcated Brits as a deconcentration area. This apartheid legislation aimed to promote economic development in outlying areas in South Africa, often on the border of small, fragmented black homelands or Bantustans. The idea was to reduce the flow of African people into white areas. Brits bordered on the homeland of Bophuthatswana, and the state offered industry generous incentives to move into this new industrial zone, including tax breaks and substantial wage subsidies.[3]

Because there were no trade unions in these zones, many of the companies allowed workers' wages and conditions to fall below survival levels. But this was a significant moment in the history of Brits, which, prior to the 1970s, had been a small, lacklustre agricultural town. Led by the auto industry – in particular Alfa Romeo, Robert Bosch and Firestone – a hub of manufacturing industries developed in the thorny bushveld, eager to take advantage of the government's seductive offers.

In 1973 National Party Prime Minister B.J. Vorster officially opened Brits's industrial area. What he had not anticipated was that this compact zone lay ripe for trade union organisation.[4] But it was not the emergent black unions which first saw these possibilities in Brits, but the youth of Oukasie, in a remarkable Roman Catholic organisation known as the Young Christian Workers (YCW).

A French priest, Jean-Marie Dumortier – J.M. to the Oukasie community – had been sent by the Catholic Church in France to establish a branch of this pro-worker organisation in Oukasie and Mothutlung in the late 1970s. His arrival marked the development of a powerful black leadership, particularly from Oukasie, both in trade unions and in the community. So strong was the YCW's impact on youth leadership that it changed the face of politics and development in Brits and Oukasie.

In order to understand why the Oukasie leadership was so effective, it is important to know how YCW recruits were trained and how they operated. It is also crucial to understand how they engaged with emerging non-racial trade unions and how they built the union movement in Brits. This chapter explores the intersection of these two forces for change and demonstrates how powerful black leaders emerged in the area.

Christianity with a worker's punch

On 12 December 1982 about 2 000 people gathered in the Cathedral Hall in Johannesburg to celebrate the centenary of Joseph Cardijn, a Belgian priest who had founded the Young Christian Workers in 1925. Archbishop Denis Hurley, who had adopted a strong anti-apartheid stance, praised the founder and his YCW followers. Then about a hundred workers stood up and raised their fists. They were dismissed workers from B&S, a Brits furniture factory, which had been organised by YCW activists and then passed on to the Metal and Allied Workers Union (MAWU).[5]

For YCW activists, the presence of workers at their meeting was nothing new nor was it accidental. After World War I Cardijn had been struck by the high levels of exploitation in his working-class neighbourhood, as well as by the demise of a Christian ethic. In response, he launched the YCW. At first, he and his new organisation clashed with the Catholic trade unions. Their patronising attitude to organising working people convinced Cardijn of the importance of an autonomous movement, owned and controlled by the youth and workers rather than by the church hierarchy. This insistence on independence continued to characterise the YCW's interactions with all civil society and political formations across the globe.[6]

By the time the International YCW was launched in 1957 it had already spread to Africa, beginning in the Belgian Congo. In the 1960s harsh repression of the YCW in Latin America, as well as the Paris 1968 student demonstrations, made it "more radical, more ideological and more political".[7] In 1975 the YCW World Council met in Linz, Austria, and emphasised the working-class nature of the movement and the need to empower young workers to claim their rights. The Declaration of Principles emerging from this meeting expressed strong anti-capitalist sentiments and called for the creation of a classless society. It declared:

> Capitalism has led to the growth of the gap between rich countries and poor countries, and indeed between the rich and poor within the countries. Technology and information are controlled by the dominant class. A small minority of rich people dominate, exploit and make decisions on behalf of a majority of people who live in poverty and constant exclusion.[8]

In poverty-stricken apartheid South Africa, such revolutionary ideas fell on fertile ground.

A few YCW groups existed in South Africa in the 1930s and 1940s but it was only in the 1950s that the movement expanded. After a year of training with the YCW in Britain, Eric Tyacke, a trade unionist and Catholic lay activist from Johannesburg, relaunched the movement in South Africa in 1949. During the 1950s and 1960s, the YCW was a church-based movement comprising about a hundred groups spread across the main cities. According to a YCW National Council report, about 65% of these groups were composed of Africans, about 20% were coloureds and the rest were white or mixed groups.[9] By this time, the YCW had become a multi-racial movement which was beginning to engage with workers' concerns. From the 1970s, Tyacke and his wife, Jean, began working in the Trade Union Council of South Africa (TUCSA), with Tyacke running its African Affairs Department.[10]

In the 1970s, when the YCW seriously took off in South Africa, it was based on an understanding that it was a youth movement grounded in Christian values and that it should be run by and for workers. It was an autonomous movement which lived by its own means. It made use of Catholic Church infrastructure such as offices and halls for meetings – the Catholic hall in Oukasie was a critical meeting place – but otherwise members contributed whatever they could and engaged in fundraising. YCW organisers were paid according to their needs. After drawing up a personal budget, a committee evaluated these needs "and it would usually get knocked down. I earned R80 per month", remembered Moses Cloete, a former general secretary of the YCW in South Africa (YCWSA) and later its international secretary.[11]

"It was non-aligned but not neutral," explained Cloete. Its independence resulted in clashes with the South African Communist Party (SACP) in the 1970s and with the United Democratic Front (UDF) in 1983 when it refused to affiliate on the grounds that the UDF's organising style was unfocused, prone to jargon and populist in orientation, relying on hyped mass mobilisation. Laughing, Cloete remembered how the UDF was viewed by YCW activists as "a bunch of lazy people who read the Freedom Charter and would come and shout". Jacob Moatshe, an Oukasie

YCW member, wrote in an email to Cloete:

> YCW was guided by very clear principles not to be involved in popular politics but to constructively criticise and help 'educate' populist ideologies. While we were detained under the emergency regulations, most comrades were arrested for wearing UDF T-shirts, or toyi-toying [doing a militant dance], but YCW *members were arrested for planning and taking actions in their own localities*... They were concerned about the realities that affected people on the ground, planned action with such people and took responsibility of such actions. That is a very clear component of the YCW as compared to popular organisations [emphasis in the original].[12]

After the June 1976 student uprising in Soweto, the YCW dedicated itself even more fervently to organising workers despite attacks on its leadership by the apartheid state. In 1978 YCW marches around the country to celebrate St Joseph the Worker Day triggered a harsh response from the state. Along with a number of worker and Christian Left organisations it came under state attack. "Kruger [Minister of Police at the time] said we were Young *Communist* Workers, not Young *Christian* Workers", recalled Cloete. Thirty national and regional leaders of the YCW were arrested, including its president, and some were charged under Section 6 of the Terrorism Act. However, while the Christian Institute was banned, there was an international outcry on behalf of the YCW. Supporters in 120 countries engaged in a campaign, picketed South African embassies, marched and wrote letters to the Pope. This resulted in the release of its leaders, although some were banned and prohibited from engaging in political activity. Eric and Jean Tyacke had already been banned for a five-year period in 1976.

In Oukasie in the late 1970s the YCW took root among six young people recruited by Jean-Marie Dumortier; these six underwent YCW training. Some of them were high school students whom the YCW recruited and trained, so that by the time they became workers they could defend themselves and their co-workers. This training converted them into radical activists. The YCW "was a parish movement; it was not dominated by priests", explained Cloete. He believed that this left space for young people to shape the organisation according to local needs.

Hlokoza Motau, a Brits YCW member and later an international relations officer of the National Union of Metalworkers of South Africa (NUMSA), recalled that the Brits YCW celebrated St Joseph the Worker Day on 1 May – a thinly veiled way for workers to celebrate May Day, which had been outlawed by the regime. In 1981, for example, they organised a march through Brits which also involved Roman Catholic cardinals, in particular Bishop Daniel from Pretoria. When attempting to break up the march, the police were confronted by Daniel who informed them that he had organised the "procession". Despite arresting a number of marchers, the police were forced to drop an "illegal gatherings" case because religious processions did not require permission.[13]

In Brits the small YCW group underwent training and started organising workers. Its organising style was based on the method of "See–Judge–Act". In essence, this meant observe, analyse and assess the issues and problems in the workplace or community, and then plan appropriate action to change things. This led to an understanding of the need for change but also allowed people to decide for themselves what action to take. Members were open to ideas and non-prescriptive in the way they operated, and they welcomed non-Christians into their activities. In Brits the YCW's way of operating greatly empowered community and trade union members.

The YCW training programme began with personal exploration, where trainees had to first reflect on what needed to be changed in their community or workplace. Thereafter they had to consider pertinent questions. Moses Cloete explained:

> So, for example, we were asked, 'Is there anything wrong if a workers' committee has lunch with the bosses?' Then at the end of every session we asked, 'What can change the situation?' and we would identify a task to perform before the next meeting. So you may decide that you will talk to five workers. Then you would continue reporting until the whole factory was organised. The training was a series of reflections and actions, and members became militant after taking action.

After training, groups continued to meet regularly to reflect, strategise and decide on activities. Sometimes the regional organiser attended and asked questions such as, "Why didn't you take the *Young Worker* [YCW newspaper] to the meeting?" and there would be discussion. Members were accountable, and as they engaged in focused activities they grew in confidence and broached more complex tasks and became organisers, trainers or leaders themselves.

"The YCW was a real university for me. I became grounded and conscientised through my own problems.

You took responsibility and became proud of your own actions," commented Jacob Moatshe.[14] This was political awareness and assuming responsibility where none had previously existed – in your cadre, at school, in the community and at work.

Some committees took on specialist activities such as writing for and distributing the *Young Worker*, which was an important organising tool. Members sold it in factories, at taxi ranks and at meetings. Every committee was encouraged to write about their activities, successes, failures, reflections and future activities. Each YCW region also had its own library, and activists were exposed to literature on the history of trade unions, Marxism and models of classless societies in countries such as Nicaragua and Tanzania.

YCW members in Brits read the *Young Worker* and learned about union activity in South Africa. Moatshe recalled other YCW members encouraging him to read political texts:

> YCW member Hlokoza Motau was an eye-opener for me. He really understood the working-class struggle. He gave me my first edition of Marx and passed on lots of other readings to me, like Martin Luther's book *Strength to Love*.

YCW and unions unite: The struggle at B&S

In 1980 the YCW launched its Genuine Representation Campaign, which Oukasie members recall as important for framing their activities both in the organisation of workers and of the community. Genuine Representation meant identifying and developing alternatives to "token" institutions in the workplace, communities and schools. The Campaign promoted independent trade unions based on workers' control as an alternative to workplace liaison committees and racially constituted parallel unions. In townships it supported the formation of democratically elected civic organisations to replace discredited state community councils and black local authorities where corrupt officials held sway. [15]

The YCW produced a manual to guide the Campaign. Its contents explored how to organise a campaign and included guidelines for pre-campaign meetings, launching of activities, rally information, ways of campaigning and songs. The manual suggested that community and worker meetings should divide into groups and plan around such questions as: Who can our group involve in the campaign in our township or area? In our schools? At work? At church? Who did we involve last year? Who do we invite to the launching weekend? How many launching pamphlets do we want? Dates were set for each phase of action, which involved detailed report-backs and discussion. Group committees were required to review the past month and plan for the next. Study methods were inclusive, imaginative and required active participation from all members in groups through song, discussion, analysing messages on T-shirts and so on. The manual was presented accessibly, with images and cartoons, and was brief and easy to read.[16]

In Brits, David Modimoeng and Peter Dantjies embraced the campaign and were soon dismissed for attempting to organise workers at Femco, a refrigeration factory where they had been employed after school. Unemployed and blacklisted by Brits's employers, they began to organise workers in the area.[17] Their efforts were soon focused on B&S, which had moved to Brits in 1969, lured by government incentives. It manufactured steel furniture and was making good profits, ranking third in the *Sunday Times* Top 100 Companies in 1981.[18] It employed 900 people, mainly women workers, who commuted long distances from dry, overcrowded villages and resettlement camps in Bophuthatswana to earn as little as R196 a month. Women were in the lowest wage categories and were paid significantly less than men in the same jobs.[19] They complained of physical assaults, verbal abuse, searches of their bodies and belongings, lack of safety equipment and a complete absence of communication with management.[20] The YCW activists encountered a hostile management who refused to talk to them or to the workers.

The YCW activists took the lead and invited metal unions affiliated to the Federation of South African Trade Unions (FOSATU) to organise in the area. Their values and ways of operating were similar. They both espoused active, accountable organisational engagement accompanied by planning, strategic reflection and assessment, while keeping a low profile to avoid the apartheid state's attention. They shared an independent organisational style which relied on critical judgement, financial independence and a suspicion of populist rhetoric. Embracing non-racism, they both held a socialist vision for a future South Africa where workers would control their own destiny. Union members built their unions, and YCW members built their organisation – the members *were* the organisation.

When they got the invitation from YCW activists to assist in organising the B&S factory, the metal unions at first hesitated as a recent defeat at Sigma in Pretoria had left their resources depleted. But YCW activists persisted and MAWU sent an organiser, Taffy Adler. Adler was working as an organiser for the National Automobile and Allied Workers' Union (NAAWU), with whom MAWU cooperated. He recalls his impression of these YCW activists:

> Exceptional people who flourished in that small environment... Its leadership was exceptionally strong and deep-rooted and that partly goes back to the early involvement of many of those leaders in YCW, which was there before the unions, and developed this core of leadership who moved into the unions and politics and the community.[21]

The early activists who first organised workers in Brits were known as the "super group" in the YCW, and David Modimoeng and Peter Dantjies were destined to make a large contribution to the union.

MAWU began organising B&S in 1982 and soon won over 70% of the workforce. The company sacked the shop stewards' committee on the pretext that it needed to retrench, but the committee was reinstated after a strike. However, B&S still refused to recognise the union. Under sustained pressure from MAWU, in September 1982 management switched off the factory's machines and dismissed its 900 workers. They were told that the factory would close for three days, and that they could apply for selective re-employment.[22] About 300 MAWU members gathered outside the gate to demand a return to work but were replaced by other workers.[23]

MAWU took the case to the industrial court on the

basis of unfair labour practice and the victimisation of union members. Thus began a year-long trial of strength during which the maintenance of solidarity was central. Ironically, this was assisted by jobs being scarce and the local employers' association ensuring the blacklisting of union members.[24]

The shop stewards' committee, assisted by YCW members, coordinated strike activity. It ensured regular meetings, a steady stream of media releases and publicity and discussions on how to sustain the families of striking workers. The 300 dismissed workers fought on in an atmosphere of "quasi-religious fervour".[25]

B&S was a family business in which members of the Back family behaved as a law unto themselves and felt personally insulted by workers' disloyalty. Taffy Adler recalls:

> The management was paternalistic ... they recruited all their domestics from B&S workers or families of B&S workers... The mother of one of the strikers was a domestic in the family's house in Johannesburg and the family would talk, so we were getting these nightly reports as to what was going to happen in the factory the next morning. It was a great intelligence system. And the family was really hurt by these people turning on them – they've been there for years, they taught them everything they knew, how could they bite the hand that fed them? At times it got quite dangerous; in particular, the one son was a bit mentally unbalanced and had a gun, and he drew that in discussions at the gate.[26]

Surviving the B&S strike
(written by a member of the B&S Committee)

Some of us had savings and we lived on these and also shared them out. Also, people in the community were initially willing to help us out...

We decided that people should report every day... We began discussing how we were harassed by management, and how workers in other factories were also harassed... We would take examples of people's experiences and get workers to talk and comment. We discovered that if we want to survive here we will have to stick together, as this will be the only way to keep the organisation strong. We spent a lot of time asking people how they felt about the dismissal – whether they thought it was unfair. Finally, we all agreed it was unfair...

We discovered it was possible to motivate the people, and not to separate ourselves from one another by being Xhosa or Tswana, finding that each and every one of us is useful to the others...

The committee planned to get help from the local churches. We got all the people involved in this by asking each one of them to take a letter to the church in their area. We also planned to get help from other workers in the area... There were a few problems when we started getting money from outside as some of the workers thought that the money would just go to the committee... We explained that we were all in the struggle. Some of us had real problems with transport, and some of the money went into making sure that those who wanted to come to the hall, could.

There were some problems, especially emergencies – people who could not pay for treatment, kids who were sick. The way we dealt with this was to all come together and make a contribution from our savings...

People were complaining that their families were putting them under a lot of pressure to go back to work ... some of us are the only member of the family with a full-time job and consequently the families had to make sacrifices. This is why we are so close now... We would send a few of the committee members to talk to the whole family and explain.

Each day we report what we have heard about the factory – many friends were working there and they tell us exactly what is going on... When two committee members were arrested under the Intimidation Act, and the charges later withdrawn, this gave us faith in the union that something could be done for us...

Some of us do not eat properly and cannot feed our children like we used to; some of us have sent our children away to our parents. Many of us had to sell our belongings, such as clothes, bicycles and watches, and some of us had goods repossessed. Some of us have had to sell our goats and cattle and this was very difficult as we sold them for very little...

People have changed through all the discussions. We have come to realise what it is to sacrifice and stick together and to trust one another – that an injury to one is an injury to all.[27]

Ellen Khoza, a staunch B&S strike committee member and later Joint Parent's Committee member (Photo: G. de Vlieg)

The company fought on for a year, resisting unionisation. Then, sensing defeat, it was sold to Gundle Industries, which settled in September 1983, before the case could go to the industrial court. The new owner reinstated workers, recognised the union and gave R200 000 towards lost pay.[28] An immense victory had been won. For Jean-Marie Dumortier this was "the beginning of justice which would emerge for the workers of Oukasie".[29] The length of the strike and the publicity surrounding it spread the union word, a process strengthened by the company's use of Bophuthatswana Radio to urge workers to return to work; this meant that everyone watched the outcome of the strike with interest.[30] Dumortier describes the response:

> I cannot recall without a tightening of my throat the meeting which followed their victory with the young militants of the YCW which had organised an end of year regional meeting. They came in buses and when their songs died away with the last buses I found myself alone in the hall, almost fainting from the strength of feeling. There are days when I think life should stop. In my head was floating this reflection of Peter [Dantjies] after he had seen a video cassette that the university team[31] had put together to commemorate the struggle of the workers.[32]

Protracted ordeals like the B&S strike taught ostensibly powerless people lessons in the exercise of power and ways of using their muscle in future battles. Levy Mamabolo, a worker from Robert Bosch in Brits, learned about MAWU through the B&S struggle and "went from one township to another wherever Bosch workers lived, to recruit. We were determined to ... force the bosses to negotiate with us."[33] Meanwhile, NAAWU was organising the Firestone factory where, in 1983, workers went on strike for a R2 per hour living wage and won. The following year workers at Alfa Romeo waged a successful wage strike, and unionisation proceeded in other factories such as Auto Cables, Chubb Fire and Afrox. Brits was fast becoming a union town.

> It was ... a time when the Trade Union was shaping itself from scratch ... from the workplace, workshop by workshop, factory by factory ... worker by worker to finally unite them and force the managements to recognize the organization their workforce had patiently and secretly developed.[34]

The shop steward leadership in these early organised factories in Brits added a further authoritative layer to the YCW leadership in Oukasie. The union movement produced such outstanding leaders as Levy Mamabolo, Marshall Buys, Peter Magagula and July Khoza to name a few, while YCW leadership skills were further sharpened in the union environment. The YCW's Peter Dantjies, David Modimoeng, Hlokoza Motau, Tshidi Mangoathe and Sello Ramakobye ultimately all joined MAWU or NAAWU. Jean-Marie Dumortier commented:

> This group of young people who joined the YCW in Oukasie ... managed to launch the Trade Unions in Brits, to the surprise of the officials of the emerging Trade Unions in Pretoria, who could not believe that they would ever be able to extend their organization that far, in such a remote area.[35]

A Brits Firestone worker making a point during a 1983 strike to demand a living wage of R2 an hour (Photo: P. Weinberg)

Union militancy in the area meant that strong and confident leadership had emerged to lead the challenge against the government from 1985 to 1989, when it attempted to move Oukasie residents to Lethlabile, 24 kilometres away. When the YCW called the first community meeting to discuss the removals, it was trade union and YCW leaders who were elected to the Brits Action Committee (BAC) that had been formed to resist the removals. Unlike many townships in South Africa at the time, the UDF and the Congress of South African Students (COSAS) were not a presence in Brits nor was the armed wing of the African National Congress (ANC), Umkhonto we Sizwe (MK). Struggles in Oukasie in the 1980s and early 1990s were conducted by community organisations, usually led by strong trade union and YCW leadership.

TWO

Oukasie Resists – "We Shall Not Be Moved!"

"As long as I can remember, Oukasie was designated to be moved," observed Japie Steenkamp, a National Party (NP) councillor in Brits from the early 1970s to the late 1990s.[36] As the town developed, however, Oukasie clung tenaciously to the white town's outer perimeter. NP councillors always considered it a "black spot" and various attempts to remove Oukasie's residents unfolded from the 1960s onwards. But the final consolidated drive came in the mid-1980s.

This chapter examines the NP government's massive efforts to eliminate Oukasie. Indeed, it was the last major urban removal endeavour by the apartheid government. The chapter also charts the community's extraordinarily tenacious battle to resist these attempts.

Early attempts at removal

In 1981 the apartheid government announced that it would no longer engage in the removals of the 1960s and 1970s where people were forcibly corralled together, trucked into the open veld and dumped. It claimed that in future people would be consulted about removals. The government was trying to project a reformist image, having realised in the face of international sanctions that it could no longer afford the negative publicity arising from brutal relocations. Going further, in 1985 the government declared an end to forced removals altogether.[37] Instead, they said, removals would be "voluntary" and the state would engage in a "winning the hearts and minds" campaign.

Such attempts to disguise the ongoing removal of black people to satisfy the needs of whites led to a haze of confused and devious government actions. The Transvaal Rural Action Committee (TRAC, a project of the Black Sash*) was sceptical; it commented in a pamphlet:

> The basic question is whether sweet-talk alone is enough to convince people to leave their homes and everything they have built up and participate in their own removal. Sweet talk seems to run out very soon in the process of persuasion.[38]

And indeed, forced removals did not end, as the government continued to pursue the relocation of over two million people.[39]

---

* The Black Sash was a non-violent white women's resistance organisation founded in 1955 in South Africa. Women wore black sashes to mourn and protest against a succession of unjust laws. The organisation ran advice offices for victims of unjust laws including pass offences. The Transvaal Rural Action Committee was a project to defend victims of forced removals.

Removals were not only about eliminating so-called black spots in white areas. More importantly, they were about legitimising the apartheid Bantustan policy. Also known as the homeland policy, government envisaged a system where each ethnic group would run its own affairs in areas that would eventually become "independent" of South Africa. Its motive behind the creation of industrial decentralised zones on the borders of homelands, as in the case of Brits, was to legitimise supposedly independent homelands such as Bophuthatswana, and to show that they were viable, could attract capital, generate employment and run successful economies. Part of the new "voluntary" form of relocation was the "incorporation process" executed under the 1980 Borders of Particular States Extension Act. This piece of legislation enabled the snipping of bits of land out of South Africa and adding them to "independent" Bantustans. At the stroke of a pen, and sometimes literally overnight, a group of African people might find themselves ruled by repressive black governments in a Bantustan. This often resulted in violent responses as people resisted losing their South African citizenship, confronting harassment, detentions and beatings at the hands of brutal homeland police. For these people, a deep hatred of the Bantustan system was born.[40]

Efforts to relocate Oukasie residents began in the early 1960s and were initially piecemeal. Some families were moved to Ga-Rankuwa (mainly created to relocate people from Lady Selborne in Pretoria) and Mabopane, where new townships had been developed. Soon after, in 1969, the government moved a number of Oukasie families to the new township of Mothutlung, 10 kilometres north-east of Brits. Hlokoza Motau, an Oukasie YCW member, recalls his family being moved there in the 1960s when they were offered a four-roomed house with internal running water and water-borne sanitation. Oukasie residents by contrast had external taps and a bucket system for sanitation. Mothutlung was created to encourage people to move from Oukasie, and many people went voluntarily although it was later incorporated into the Bophuthatswana homeland.[41]

Later, in the early 1970s, some families who were unable to secure permits to reside in Oukasie drifted off to Soshanguve, another recently declared township where electricity, water and housing title deeds were granted. Also in the 1970s, a number of Oukasie families were moved to Hartebeesfontein, an underdeveloped area about 25 kilometres from Brits. People with permanent jobs in Brits tended to remain in Oukasie.[42]

1985: Final push for removal

A decade later, on 7 December 1985, the government again declared its intention to remove people from Oukasie. But this time its ambitions were much larger – it hoped to relocate all of Oukasie's 15 000 residents. It proposed moving people to Lethlabile, 25 kilometres from Brits. Lethlabile was a newly built township offering household water, stands or houses on stands, electricity, tarred roads, water-borne sewerage and other community amenities. Oukasie, on the other hand, was a ramshackle settlement of mainly self-built brick or zinc houses, often with yard tenants. Although it was set among an abundance of lush green trees, the settlement had rutted gravel roads, bucket sewerage, 54 taps at central points to serve the whole community and no electricity. Richard Stengel described

Oukasie's houses at that time:

> Most of the houses in Oukasie are metal shacks: four zinc walls topped by a flat roof of corrugated iron... People use the flat roof as a storage area... The tops are piled high – with loops of barbed wire and planks of wood, bricks, tires, parts of bicycles and baby carriages, shoes and suitcases... The objects serve another purpose: holding the roof down. Others use large stones ... placed like paperweights... Many houses have some touch of decoration: a cactus plant by the door, a rock garden, pieces of tile arranged in a pattern. Clotheslines are strung across front yards. Hung with bright fabrics, red, yellows, cobalt blues, they provide a touch of gaiety... Coal is used for heating and cooking. Mounds of it, like drifts of black snow are stored in front yards. At dusk the air of Oukasie is smudged; a cloud of smoke hovers a few feet above the township.[43]

Why was the state so intent on removing Oukasie at a time when it was seeking to project a reform image and to move away from high apartheid policies?

The most immediate reason, as the town newspaper expressed it, was that "the Brits location has been a local eyesore and abuts one of our smart suburbs".[44] Oukasie lay alongside the new white suburb of Elandsrand, developed in the mid-1970s to accommodate a rapidly increasing white population which had accompanied industrialisation in Brits. This gave renewed impetus to efforts to remove Oukasie. Sello Selepe, a unionist and Oukasie resident, commented:

Water runs down an Oukasie alleyway in the 1980s. (Photo: G. de Vlieg)

> I remember seeing an interview on SABC [South African Broadcasting Corporation], and people were saying Oukasie must be removed to stop blacks stealing white kids' bicycles and house-breaking. The Nats mobilised the white community and we had no contact with them.[45]

Oukasie was not of course the first location to be erased and its people moved to a more "modern" township. Many such removals had occurred from the 1960s onwards. The authorities began to develop townships to replace what they saw as African transient settlements.[46] Leslie Banks argues that the government's racial modernism aimed to re-engineer urban areas by offering Africans a vision of black suburbia with brick houses to live in. This policy, however, denied the right to ownership and any expression

A resident of the white suburb of Elandsrand across the road from Oukasie. Oukasie needed to be eliminated to make way for its expansion. (Photo: G. de Vlieg)

of individuality. The new townships were based on a male-centred, nuclear family, and the independent women who brewed beer and ran shebeens were flushed out. The new model drew on the authoritarian tradition of "obedience, compliance and feelings of sameness" where everyone was allocated the same house and yard size. The house was to become the instrument of discipline. Lethlabile was such a township.

Removal and swing to the right

By the early 1980s the drive to eliminate Oukasie was driven by another force as well: the rise of the ultra-right Conservative Party (CP). Led by Andries Treurnicht, the CP was formed in 1982 as a breakaway from the ruling Nationalists. It drew support chiefly from Afrikaner farmers in rural areas and towns who vehemently opposed Prime Minister P.W. Botha's reforms, which they viewed as heralding the end to white rule. The CP became the official opposition in the whites-only parliament in the 1987 elections when it surpassed the liberal-leaning Progressive Federal Party (PFP). In the 1987 local elections it won 60 municipalities, mainly in the Transvaal and Orange Free State, and received 43% of the Afrikaner vote. In the last whites-only general election in 1989, the CP increased its majority; it won 31.52% of the white electorate and 41 seats in the House of Assembly.[47]

In Brits and its surrounds, Afrikaner factionalism and parties to the right of the NP had long existed. In the early 1970s the Herstigte Nasionale Party (HNP) had wooed Brits's Afrikaans-speaking voters. It advocated strict racial segregation and Afrikaans as the only official language. Under the leadership of Jaap Marais it won a number of by-elections, and in 1981 it nearly defeated the NP candidate in Brits. However, its decline after that allowed the Conservative Party to fill the gap to the right of the reformist Nationalists. "Treurnicht was more pragmatic, more open to negotiation and more approachable in politics than the HNP," commented former Brits CP mayor Dr Bert Botha.[48] At least 75% of Brits HNP members joined the CP. Botha recalled:

> My father was an HNP member. They were more brutal in their approach than the Conservatives. The HNP members felt Treurnicht had killed the HNP and its chances of becoming the official opposition. It was a

Judas coat and there was some truth in this. There was bad feeling between them, and they broke up each other's meetings.

Botha remembers counting votes as a young student in November 1983. The National Party had called a "Yes/No" referendum to test the white population's support for a Tricameral Parliament. This gave limited powers to coloureds and Indians, with a white chamber having the power to veto their decisions. It would be accompanied by black local authority township governance and by citizenship and political participation for the majority African population in ethnic Bantustans.

South African local government income in white areas was generated chiefly through rates, payment for services, taxes and small grants from national and provincial government for specific infrastructure. Commerce and industry contributed large amounts to this.[49] Brits's white areas profited from the growth of industry under the government's decentralisation policy, and also benefitted from the enormous disparity in expenditure on the minority white areas in contrast to the majority black townships and villages which the NP minimally serviced. Black local councils were impoverished and tried to squeeze payment for services from local residents who overwhelmingly rejected the system and viewed black councillors as sell-outs.

The CP campaigned for a "No" vote because it objected to any kind of reform. However, the "Yes" vote won the referendum, and in 1984 Dr Botha joined the CP in Brits. The NP policy of "one man one vote" in South Africa, although in a very undemocratic form, was an abomination to the CP. Instead, they wanted a constellation of southern

African states, each with its own government that had partial self-rule, modelled on the United States federation of states. "It could never have worked," remarked Botha laconically. "The Nationalists had a one man one vote policy and we [the CP] said this would bring black majority rule – and this happened."

The rise of the far right alarmed the NP. The Brits Member of Parliament, Dr Jan Grobler, was afraid he would lose his seat and pushed hard for Oukasie's removal.[50] The CP was also calling loudly for Oukasie's removal and for Lethlabile's incorporation into Bophuthatswana.

In 1985 the NP used the local black councillors to announce to the people of Oukasie that they would be removed to Lethlabile. But that did not stop the rightward swing in Brits. In 1987 the Brits CP candidate Andrew Gerber won a seat in Parliament, and in 1988 the CP won an outright majority in the Brits municipality (seven CP to two NP councillors) as a white rightward swing engulfed the region. Other smaller right-wing groups such as the HNP, the Afrikaner Volksweg and the neo-fascist paramilitary Afrikaner Weerstandsbeweging (AWB) also vociferously opposed Nationalist reforms.

Japie Steenkamp was one of the two opposing Nationalists on the Brits council. He speculated that Brits was particularly prone to the formation of far-right groupings:

> I believe that Afrikaans farmers from smallholdings who were battling to make a living were not very positive, they were hard-bitten, they were not successful... These people started working at the Atomic Energy Board, Pelindaba, and they sat on the bus for one and half hours every

morning and evening, and they aired all their aggravation, they brewed it up. They got into a bad habit of sitting and cursing and complaining ... and heated each other up.

For local black people, however, it did not really matter whether the Conservatives or the NP were in power. As former Firestone head shop steward Sello Ramakobye commented:

> Farmers were used to getting away with murder and not tolerating opposition from black people. In the 1970s you could not walk on the same pavement as a white lady in Brits, and it only started to change in the early 1980s. Also, there were strict separate queues and sometimes entrances for blacks and whites in all shops, the post office and so on.[51]

Sirens were used at night so that all black people, except for domestic workers, would leave Brits town. The Brits municipal police and the Special Branch used to look for people, particularly in the rooms of domestic workers, to see if they were breaking the law.[52]

Jacob Moatshe commented in an interview that the desire by the ultra-right to get rid of Oukasie was also driven by the fear of a "proletarian revolutionary struggle of highly unionised workers taking place on the white town's doorstep."[53] Anti-labour feeling was running high, and in the beginning companies either overtly supported removals or passively watched government actions unfold. Sello Ramakobye recalls that Firestone gave loans to people who wanted houses in Lethlabile, and that companies provided transport for goods and furniture to be moved to the new township.

The state's strategy for removals

A TRAC pamphlet charts a common pattern in the state's approach to removals in the mid-1980s. The first step was state officials informing the community about the removal, followed by a divide-and-rule strategy whereby the state consulted selected people and offered them perks to move. If divide-and-rule failed, the second stage was to impose restrictions in the targeted area, such as the prohibition of community meetings to plan a response. This would often be accompanied by the withdrawal of state services in order to create deteriorating slum conditions which would result in some people moving away in desperation. If worsening conditions did not drive people out, the state went on to the third stage. They threatened force, and a waiting game ensued. Finally, if the community still held out, the fourth step was an escalation of violence.[54] More details are given below, but that is basically what happened in Oukasie.[55]

First stage of removal: Carrot, stick and community response

In 1976 the government had bought about 4 000 hectares of land across from the Bophuthatswana border near Maboloka. There, they planned to establish Lethlabile. By 1982 it had spent over R20 million to develop Lethlabile – an average cost of R6 380 per plot. In 1985 the state announced to Oukasie's 15 000 residents through its community councillors that there were new houses available in Lethlabile into which 350 families could immediately move.[56] People were also told that they could no longer build new houses in Oukasie. Sam Khumalo, the mayor, led by example and moved to Lethlabile. Jacob Moatshe recalls:

> Mack Tjale was an influential shop owner who became a councillor. Ndlovu was principal of a school. George Mopedi was a shebeen and shop owner and ran an ambulance service. They were all members of the black local authority who moved [to Lethlabile] and influenced people to move.

The day after the council announced its intention to get rid of Oukasie, YCW activists came together to organise a community response. Caleb Dube, a community activist, recalls:

> I belonged to the anti-removal committee in Oukasie… YCW organised a no-removal meeting … at the RC church; we were 15 people. We organised student committees – young guys – to collect 50 cents from each house, house by house, to be able to get a lawyer. And this is how we spread the message of the removal. The following week the hall was so full, and we elected an anti-removal committee.[57]

The political climate in South Africa had changed since the Mothutlung removals in the 1960s. From 1976 onwards, people across the country had risen up to reject apartheid's reformist policies. Oukasie residents felt the effects of this feverish revolt and at least 800 residents attended the meeting and rejected the removal. A 12-member executive consisting chiefly of trade unionists and YCW members was elected to the Brits Action Committee (BAC). It was chaired by Marshall Buys, formerly a member of the National Automobile and Allied Workers' Union (NAAWU); he had been fired in the 1983 Firestone strike. Moatshe recalls what he said to the meeting that day:

> They were destined to be removed, and jobs would be lost; there would be no unions. I portrayed a scenario which identified with the struggle in general in South Africa. I told people about the efforts of the Black Sash, TRAC, the Justice and Peace Commission in the Catholic Church with Father Smangaliso Mkhatshwa and Bishop Daniel. We used Chippa Mongalo in Happy Hearts, a soccer star, and I told them he is not going to move. This club became very important in the struggle. And burial societies.

Union leaders, current and former, became the leaders of the struggle against the removals. They had "learnt their politics from a decade of acquiring power on the shop floor. They were tough, pragmatic, and experienced."[58] The shop stewards saw no division between the community and shop-floor struggles, and many workers came from Oukasie. Marshall Buys commented:

> The unions have never limited themselves to direct bargaining; they were always part of the struggle as a whole. We didn't have political organisation in Oukasie. The unions had to do something. If it were not for the concern of the unions, we already might have been dragged away.[59]

Over the next few months the BAC collected over 4 000 signatures protesting the removal.[60] Powerful activists emerged, some of who were not on the committee. They included Malasba Lazarus Mangoathe from B&S, who Moatshe remembers as being "a cornerstone of the movement – a very honest and active person." Despite the resistance, by early 1986 about 4 000 people had moved to Lethlabile.[61] They were awarded compensation of between R5 000 and R10 000 for their Oukasie houses, which were frequently demolished and their numerous tenants forced out.

Oukasie's days are numbered: houses with numbers were marked for demolition. (Photo: G de Vlieg)

Ironically, Caleb Dube, who sat on the Oukasie anti-removal committee, was one of the early people to move to Lethlabile. He worked at Afrox in Brits's industrial zone and was an active member of the Steel Engineering and Allied Workers' Union of South Africa (SEWUSA). It was a member of the Trade Union Council of South Africa

Malasba Lazarus Mangoathe, a staunch anti-removal activist, working at his small shoe-repair business (Photo: G. de Vlieg)

(TUCSA) and was headed by Jane Hlongwane, a YCW member. Dube studied and received a diploma from the Project Management Institute. After that, he was noticed by management for his leadership potential and was promoted to supervisor and then to production foreman. This meant he was promoted out of the bargaining unit and had to resign from the union. In a militant trade union environment, members felt he had been "bought" by management.

> I showed them the union constitution to prove this was not the case… Union members living in Oukasie started talking, and I was going home to my kids and knowing it was a very tense situation as people suspected I was a sell-out. My kids were at home and I was doing night

shift. It was very tough for me. I was a founder member of the anti-removal committee but I felt unsafe and that my family were unsafe.

Management urged him to move out of Oukasie for safety reasons, as did his wife and uncle, who was a councillor who "sided with the system". He went to a Sunday viewing of stands in Lethlabile. In Zone 1 the state offered four-roomed houses but in Zones 2, 8 and 10 serviced stands were provided. Dube chose to build his own house and the following Monday he bought a double stand for R52 each. The state awarded him R5 000 remuneration for the house he had built in Oukasie and this allowed him to purchase bricks. Afrox assisted him with a home loan from their housing scheme of R10 000 at a 7% interest rate to be paid off over three years. After that, a further loan was granted.

When the government saw that people were moving into Lethlabile, it began to construct tarred roads. Some moved voluntarily; others were moved in coercive ways. Township officials would visit women in Oukasie when their husbands were absent and persuade or intimidate them into moving. Sello Ramakobye recalls that, "my wife had a friend who moved while her husband was at work. They never reconciled. It broke up their marriage."

Other women, however, became strong, independent participants in the anti-removal struggle. School principal and later Madibeng councillor Caroline Mashike remembers that she "attended meetings where I became a strong and a good leader. I could think on my own, make decisions. It was free education. We had meetings during the week and on weekends."[62]

Caleb Dube outside his Lethlabile house (Photo: K. Forrest)

Reasons for resisting removal to Lethlabile

By August 1986 the move to Lethlabile had stagnated, and remaining Oukasie residents showed no sign of leaving. There were several reasons why they refused to move.

Too far from work

Although Caleb Dube describes buying a plot for almost nothing and also receiving compensation for his house in Oukasie, it was only the early movers who received this kind of benefit. In a departure from the 1960s removals, the state permitted people in Lethlabile to purchase land and receive title deeds. They could also design and build their own homes, which many preferred to do. Inevitably, wealthier, professional and educated Oukasie residents such as teachers and businessmen moved to Lethlabile. Others opted for very reasonably priced rental stock, but many simply could not afford the daily cost of transport from Lethlabile to Brits when Oukasie lay within quick walking distance to work.

Also many people were unemployed, and from Oukasie they could easily walk into the town to seek work. For many this was a daily ritual. A major blow had been the closure of the Alfa Romeo factory in 1985 when hundreds of workers lost their jobs. If they were stuck 20 kilometres away in Lethlabile, walking to town would be impossible. This was a major reason for people not to move.

Fear of incorporation into Bophuthatswana

Oukasie residents also expressed deep fears of Lethlabile being incorporated into the Bophuthatswana Bantustan. They had observed trade union and other repression there, as well as heavy taxation by homeland authorities. Bophuthatswana had introduced the Industrial Conciliation Act in 1983, but to achieve union recognition the head office of the union had to be based in the Bantustan. This made it difficult for South Africa's unions to organise there. Further, according to the Internal Security Act, no more than 20 people could meet, and union organisers were arrested for holding illegal gatherings. At the same time, a complicated conciliation process made it almost impossible to strike.[63]

In 1986 Bophuthatswana police conducted a brutal campaign against South African unionists living in the Bantustan and commuting to work. Many were beaten, whipped, or arrested and tortured.[64]

People also witnessed the ferocity with which Bantustan police attacked those who resisted incorporation into the homeland. Resistance to the homeland system was deeply political, as African people struggled for their right to be full citizens of South Africa and not just citizens of fragmented homelands.

Jacob Moatshe recalls a sympathetic Pretoria-based law firm taking a case for him against the Minister of Law and Order when the state tried to force him to apply for homeland citizenship: "I was picked up by police who attempted to throttle me because I would not carry a pass book or take Bop [Bophuthatswana] citizenship." Moatshe also remembers that in 1984 teachers at Tsogo School in Mmakau in the district of Ga-Rankuwa in the homeland, where he taught, were instructed to teach history from a book glorifying the Bantustan. He refused and instead taught an alternative South African history. This meant that he was an immediate target when the South African police later asked the homeland police to detain him.

TRAC was waging removal struggles in other parts of the Transvaal, and Oukasie residents heard about Moutse's challenge to incorporation in the homeland of KwaNdebele. They also came into contact with the Bakwena ba Magopa, who were fighting relocation from Ventersdorp, 120 kilometres from Brits, and they saw how in 1984 Braklaagte in the western Transvaal was incorporated into Bophuthatswana.[65] All this made them more determined not to move to Lethlabile.

Their resolute stand meant that the government feared that Oukasie residents' rejection of incorporation would lead to further resistance to removals. In early 1986 the South African government persuaded Bophuthatswana's

Chief Minister Lucas Mangope that Lethlabile should not be absorbed into the homeland.[66] This was a quiet, indirect victory by Oukasie residents.

People's opposition to being incorporated meant that Oukasie became the centre of resistance to homeland policy in the area. The YCW had developed some leadership in neighbouring Mothutlung and Ga-Rankuwa, of which Pat Makhura was the most prominent. But, as Jacob Moatshe remembers, "It was very difficult to mobilise in the homeland, so Oukasie people were at the forefront and they came to meetings at the church here."

Moatshe recalls his fear of organising in the homelands, which resulted from a 1989 YCW National Council meeting in Zone 5 in a local church in Ga-Rankuwa. Some comrades were wearing revolutionary T-shirts which were banned in Bophuthatswana, as was trade union clothing. On the first night the church was surrounded by Bophuthatswana military and police carrying guns. Ironically, they were led by General Mmokobyane, who had long lived in Oukasie. Moatshe described the situation they faced:

> They swore at us ... we were trembling. The police wore helmets and they were from Taung in the far north-west, not local, very rural and trained by Koevoet.* We prayed with a prayer group that was there from Soweto, and we pretended we were with them. We were addressed by the General who called us terrorists. The Eastern Cape comrades left the next day, they were so terrified. Political associations were banned in Bop [Bophuthatswana] and Radio Bop was very powerful and many people listened to it.

---

* Koevoet was a former South African military unit that was deployed in South West Africa, now Namibia. See Chapter 3 for more information about Koevoet.

Oukasie, a bonded community

Perhaps the overriding reason for many residents resisting removal was simply a strong sense of place. Many had been born in Oukasie. It was a strong community and the social ties were very close.

Oukasie had existed for 50 years, and although there had been continuous movement of people into the location from other places seeking jobs and wanting to be near work, people had made lives and forged strong religious and social networks.

Tshidi Mangoathe, a community activist, and Jacob Moatshe, for example, both emphasised the bonds between people in the location, including a strong identification with its soccer teams. Moatshe explained:

> There was Brits Morning Stars in their green gear; my father was a founder... Then there was Happy Hearts in their maroon outfits, with hearts on the front of their shirts, who was the main opposition. And Hotspurs in their white gear, Corians and the Bakwena with their crocodile symbol. Vuka Swallows. All from villages in Bop. We played teams from all over, like the Kellis from Pretoria.

Moatshe went on to tell how the BAC involved prominent people from the community to create cohesion in the removal struggle – people from soccer teams (such as Chipa Mongalo), shebeens and unions.

Tshidi Mangoathe was a member of the YCW and the Metal and Allied Workers Union (MAWU). She later became mayor of Madibeng (as Brits was renamed). For

Young men playing guitar in an Oukasie yard. Oukasie had a strong sense of community. (Photo: G. de Vlieg)

her, Oukasie was an important home. Her family had been forcibly moved from a small village in the north-west before she was of school-going age. When her parents found work in Natalspruit on the East Rand, she was brought to live with an aunt in Oukasie. She attended Grade 1 at Fafung near Jericho but was later moved and forced to repeat the year when her parents sought work in Vereeniging and could not prove that she had completed the grade. Unable to get a permit to live in Evaton, her parents stayed on a farm until the police arrested her father and endorsed him out by stamping his pass book to his so-called home of Fafung.

Instead of going there, though, her family simply settled in Oukasie, where she attended Grade 3. Her father took her out of school early, "because my father said I could write my name". [67] For Mangoathe, who was "angry

A People's Park created by the community (Photo: G. de Vlieg)

when we left Evaton and all our furniture – my mother only took our clothes", Oukasie was the only stable home she knew. And the YCW, "which instilled a lot of faith in me", was another kind of home. MAWU at Auto Cable where she worked, and her contact with TRAC, which educated through workshops and field trips, were her only real school. When confronted by the prospect of forced removal again, this time from Oukasie, her immediate response was to resist: "For me the issue of removal was opening up old wounds."

Mangoathe's experience of constantly having to move was not unusual for black people in South Africa. The Group Areas Act wrought havoc in people's lives. As Japie Steenkamp noted, "At this stage removals were a common thing. We [the NP] didn't work through negotiations." The area that Mangoathe's family came from in the north-west was highly unstable, and individuals being endorsed out of cities back to the rural areas was commonplace. Added to this, the NP practice of gerrymandering* within chieftainships led to severe strife between the followers of genuine traditional leaders and those who had been appointed. For example, in the Brits area the Maboloka conflict led to deep land conflict and divisions within the Bataung grouping. The Bataung were also in conflict with the minority Bafokeng. They forced the Bafokeng to pay R80 for a pass to work in Brits's industrial areas.[68] Maboloka residents fled to Oukasie during this conflict, only to be hounded by police because they lacked a township permit.

One way or the other, quite a few of Oukasie's residents had been forced to move during their lifetimes. For many of them, moving again was simply out of the question.

Second stage of removal: State restrictions and community response

When the divide-and-rule strategy only partially succeeded in removing Oukasie residents, the state began to impose restrictions.

It first banned a BAC meeting in February 1986. However, residents continued to hold their meetings in the Catholic Church hall in Oukasie. Police were unable to move legally onto this private property, so they threw tear gas into the hall causing injury, chaos and fear.

The BAC had decided not to get involved in politics.

---

* The National Party removed chiefs who resisted government policies and appointed traditional leaders sympathetic to its aims. This sometimes entailed redrawing the boundaries of the areas within which the chiefs exercised authority.

Because of this, they did not affiliate to the United Democratic Front (UDF) or any other organisation, as they believed government would find any excuse to smash it. This does not mean they were apolitical. Marshall Buys, for example, had been involved in a boycott against schooling in Afrikaans following the 1976 riots in Soweto. The school was burned down; he was charged and received eight lashes, a month in detention and was expelled from school.[69] Sello Ramakobye attributes this approach to the workerist [as opposed to populist]* position of the Federation of South African Trade Unions (FOSATU) where workers:

> learned about the banning of SACTU [South African Congress of Trade Unions] in 1966 because of its high-profile relationship with the ANC. We maintained our independence – and that the workers' struggle is different from the general political struggle, as the workers' struggle will still continue after the ANC comes to power. There were many shop stewards on the BAC committee. Of course, it did not help us from being attacked anyway in the end but it bought us some time.

The BAC continued to build support for its anti-removal campaign. The YCW comrades had been building its organisation in Oukasie in the early 1980s, and it now

---

* The "workerists" did not engage in popular politics, believing that worker power needed to be built before engaging overtly in politics. In this way, they believed, their organisation would not attract attention and be smashed by the government. They were not apolitical but believed in deferring engagement with politics until they had acquired sufficient strength to resist state attacks and promote a workers' agenda. The "populists" engaged openly in resisting government policies and mobilised particularly in townships through various organisations often affiliated to the UDF and sympathetic to the ANC.

used the leadership that had emerged. Their first successful struggle had been in 1981 when they formed the Lodger's Permit Committee. With the help of the Black Sash, they challenged the township permit system and succeeded in getting it abolished. YCW's Hlokoza Motau recalls the routine fear that this system had brought into people's lives:

> You had to have a permit to live in Oukasie and you had to pay the local administration every month to keep up the permit – even for kids. You had to have permission to stay in the township. People went to sleep in the mountains around Brits if they had no permit because of nightly raids by township police. I remember my uncle was in the middle of drinking a cup of tea when the police came in and got him. You were forced to pay a fine if you were arrested.

Sello Selepe remembers his mother sleeping in a large drum outside the house for fear of these house-by-house raids. The hated township councillors reported residents without permits to the police.

The YCW consciously strategised to include older, more experienced members of the community in their campaigns. "We struggled to get parents and the older generation to meetings even though we had invited them," said Jacob Moatshe. Parents had contributed money to the building of Botlhabelo High School in Oukasie, and some of them sat on the school board together with local councillors to administer the school funds. The YCW used the fact that these councillors seldom reported back on the school's finances to create a sense of grievance among parents. Jacob Moatshe commented, "Parents listened to us

Sello Ramakobye, a head shop steward at Firestone and an Oukasie activist whose house was firebombed (Photo: G. de Vlieg)

as I was a teacher and most YCW people had matric level and parents were also active in unions." Ellen Khoza (also on the B&S strike committee), Levy Mamabolo, Nankie Matlhare (a trade unionist), Annah Mokhari and David Madumo were a few of the respected people who responded to the YCW's queries and who then later formed the Joint Parents Committee.[70] When the YCW learned about the government's intention to remove Oukasie residents, they invited these parents to a meeting on the pretext of discussing school finance issues. The removal was on the agenda, and in this way the YCW was able to pull these influential parents into the anti-removal campaign.

The presence of large numbers of unionists living in Oukasie meant that the link between union and community was easily forged. Skills that had been learned in organising factories were rapidly applied to township struggles, and leadership crossovers occurred almost seamlessly.

Small victories, like removing the permit system, were a huge encouragement to what had formerly been a disempowered community. So when the decision to fight the removals was taken, there was already a sense that victories could be won through organisation. The BAC incorporated the members of the Parents Committee, which dissolved and provided an experienced layer of community leadership to the organisation. As Sello Selepe remarked: "We did not rely on one individual; if you were detained there were others."

The TRAC pamphlet noted:

> If the community crumbles at first attempt to divide it, the removal issue is lost in a confusion of 'leadership splits' and 'tribal disputes' and 'voluntary removals'... In many cases it [government] succeeds in dividing communities by bribing and manipulating leaders ... and the question of whether to resist or collaborate splits families down the middle... Once the leaders have agreed to move ... the resisters ... are utterly insecure.[71]

The YCW and trade unionists, with their keen strategic sense, recognised that strong leadership and sustaining community unity was absolutely critical in their anti-removal struggle. The YCW, for example, used meetings and union actions to identify community leaders. Hlokoza Motau recollects doing this during the Robert Bosch three-day sleep-in strike (*siyalala*) for a R3 an hour living wage. Women from the community organised food and blankets for 350 workers at the factory.

One of the great strengths of the Oukasie removal struggle was the active role of women. The BAC's manner of organisation was inclusive of all segments of the community and women felt at home in it. Tshidi Mangoathe, Ellen Khoza, Wanda Makgale and Nankie Matlhare had the task of organising women. They drew significant women leadership and membership into the Oukasie Women's Movement. TRAC invited the organisation to Gazankulu for training in food gardening, and here they joined with women fighting removals in Moutse and Matatiele. The Women's Movement created a strong sense of community purpose as they started crèches, laboured in joint backyard gardening, fixed roads by loading wheelbarrows with rocks and filling holes and made "wonder boxes" to keep food warm for meetings.

Tshidi Mangoathe recalls:

> We focused on the women to explain the disadvantages of moving and to know their rights. And the Black Sash assisted us to take a stand against domestic violence – there was so much domestic violence. Some women were very vocal, like Wanda Makgale.

Taking place at the same time as the relocation struggle, and cementing people even further, was the union activity continuing at workplaces such as ATC, Auto Cable, Autocast, Lumex, Roche, Dubigeon, Regbody, Edgars and R&H, where strikes and dismissals were often fought with community support. Meanwhile, union leaders solicited the help of "educated" employers and employer organisations in the anti-removal campaign. Unionists exposed Firestone, for example, for donating a large amount of money to a day care centre in Lethlabile, forcing it to withdraw the donation.[72]

BAC meetings were vibrant affairs and singing was an important glue when residents came under extreme pressure, especially when the state began withdrawing services. Jacob Moatshe remembers Jacob "Commodore" Magakwe from B&S leading the crowd in animated freedom songs:

> At meetings we sang anti-removal songs like 'We shall, we shall not be moved. / Just like a tree standing in the water, / the union is behind us, / we shall not be moved. / We will stand together. / We are black and white together.'* And the song about [Minister of Constitutional Development] Chris Heunis – 'Ons gaan nie daar nie. / Ons is hier om to bly. / Stop killing us. / Lethlabile ons gaan nie daar nie.'**
> … 'Nkosi Sikelela' was also popular; we popularised it.***

The BAC could not have survived without church support. The role of the Catholic Church and of Jean-Marie Dumortier in particular has already been outlined. "JM [Jean-Marie] was arrested and not supported by other priests. He sat in endless meetings with us," recalled Hlokoza Motau. The South African Council of Churches (SACC) established a Covenant programme to focus on the many people who were victims of forced removals and

---

* Through YCW networks Oukasie people had learned this traditional American negro spiritual song which was adapted by activists in the 1930s.

** 'We are not going there. / We are here to stay'. Songs were sung in a variety of languages such as Setswana, Afrikaans and English. The struggle in Oukasie was non-racial and inclusive.

*** "Nkosi Sikelela iAfrika", now the national anthem of South Africa, was outlawed at the time as a symbol of the banned ANC but was widely sung at struggle meetings across the country.

to lend support. This brought together different churches, and in Oukasie a committee was set up chiefly by Uniboy Hlongwane who was detained under the State of Emergency in 1988 and who died soon after being released.* [73] The programme enabled a number of BAC members to travel overseas to publicise the Oukasie removals, and also to campaign for Nelson Mandela's release and the boycott of South African goods. Motau commented:

> After a while the state was scared to move against Oukasie, as it became very high-profile internationally. Church organisations particularly publicised the removal overseas, especially the German churches... I was sent to Germany in a church group with Marshall Buys and we also went to the US.

Important also in the BAC's struggle was the help it got from supportive human rights organisations staffed with skilled and determined black and white activists. The Black Sash, TRAC and the Legal Resources Centre (LRC) in Johannesburg and Pretoria had members like Geoff Budlender, Joanne Yawitch, Sheena Duncan, Alan Morris, Lydia Kompe, Marj Brown, Aninka Claasens and Arthur Chaskalson. At the same time, strong trade unionists such as Bernie Fanaroff and Taffy Adler in MAWU and NAAWU also entered the fray.

---

* Hlongwane was first detained under the Terrorism Act, and then detained in 1986 and 1988 under the State of Emergency. Oukasie residents suspected he had been poisoned. He showed symptoms of something similar to jaundice, which turned his eyes yellow for months. Unemployed, he was unable to afford a doctor. Moatshe described him thus: "He was very committed to the struggle and chose a life in Oukasie after his middle-class parents departed. Unemployed and struggling, he sometimes went without food and depended on his comrades."

Observers have sometimes been puzzled as to why certain whites opposed apartheid, sometimes to the point of great discomfort and danger, which was not in their own interests. Amartya Sen describes the motivation of such activists very well:

> There is nothing contrary to reasoning to do things that are not entirely self-serving... Arguments that do not draw on the perspective of mutual benefit but concentrate instead on unilateral obligations because of an asymmetry of power ... can be seen in early attempts to recognise the implications of valuing the freedoms – and correspondingly human rights – for all.[74]

External activists were impressed with Oukasie's leadership. They drew the local leaders into other land struggles, which raised their consciousness of what was happening across South Africa and allowed them to forge important solidarity links. Caleb Dube recalls that the Black Sash put the BAC in touch with the Alexandra removal committee. He travelled to Johannesburg with Jacob Moatshe, and "we began to see there was a pattern of removals and we formed a network." Moatshe recalls, "When Alex township was reprieved it gave us a beacon of hope... We created a coalition with other movements in Ventersdorp, Moutse – all of which was coordinated by TRAC." Tshidi Mangoathe felt she learned a great deal from Lydia Kompe, former Transport and General Workers' unionist and TRAC organiser, with whom she travelled and witnessed removal struggles elsewhere.

One of the BAC's tactics was a legal one. Moshe Mahlaela, BAC treasurer and former NAAWU shop steward from Alfa Romeo, was left homeless when his father moved to Lethlabile. He applied for permission to build on a vacant lot and was told by Oukasie superintendent M.B. de Beer to "take this letter and go to your lawyer and tell him to stuff it up his ass..."[75] In January 1986 the LRC took the case to the Transvaal Supreme Court to order De Beer to allocate Mahlaela a site. He won the case and Geoff Budlender used this to urge the minister responsible, Chris Heunis, not to disestablish Oukasie. He reminded the minister of the government's promise to end forced removals. Two weeks later the Central Transvaal Development Board gave Mahlaela a house, and other successful applications followed. Business – including the Steel and Engineering Industries Federation of South Africa (SEIFSA, the employer organisation in the metal sector), the Federated Chamber of Industry (FCI) and the Northern Transvaal Chamber of Commerce – responded by declaring support for Oukasie residents, while the Brits Industrial Association offered to help fund upgrading in the community.

This legal victory infuriated local whites. When the government's Minister of Information attempted to address a meeting in Brits, he was shouted down for an hour by right-wing groups.[76] The stage was set for a Conservative Party victory.

Third stage of removal: The use of terror

Faced by this stubborn community resistance, the state invoked the threat of force. A waiting game began. The presence of the police and army roaming the location was intimidating. (The army was there because its barracks lay along the road to Lethlabile.) However, all that cemented people's solidarity and determination. In response, the state adopted its next strategy: a reign of terror. This began with the petrol-bombing of the Catholic Church hall frequently used by unions and community groups for planning meetings and report-backs. After that, there were personal attacks on activists' homes. The houses of Marshall Buys and Jacob Moatshe were firebombed on the night of 7 March 1986. Three nights later Sello Ramakobye's house was bombed, and the home of BAC activist Leonard Brown's parents was hit by a grenade. Fear gripped the community, and some moved.

Terror also gripped the whole country as townships nationally tilted towards general insurrection. Emboldened by an atmosphere of chaos, vigilantes bombed BAC activist and MAWU organiser David Modimoeng's house on the night of 28 May 1986, soon after his return from a Bosch strike meeting. Modimoeng gave testimony at a Truth and Reconciliation Commission (TRC) hearing in 1997:

> ... because we were at the threat of being forced-removed, as I knew that I'm an activist ... when I sleep, I will take the corrugated iron and put them on the windows ... and from there upwards I put wood.
>
> At 2 o'clock, I didn't even hear this corrugated iron falling. The hand grenade was thrown inside the house, where I was sleeping with ... my wife, and Gladys who was eight months old, and Miriam ... my wife woke me up... To reduce its strength ... I should throw a blanket on top of that bomb... That didn't help me at all... I heard a loud bang, then I screamed, because I didn't know what was happening... During that confusion ... I looked at the

roof; there was no corrugated irons, there was no roof. The three sides of the house fell on the ground.

What came to my mind, is that I must take these children before their mother and take them outside. I was able to take the two children outside... Then I sat next to the bed and shook her to wake up. She didn't reply... I was not aware that the shrapnel from that bomb went to my feet and my feet, my leg is damaged... I stayed in the hospital for 13 days, and my wife was in the mortuary ... when I was recovering, I couldn't bury my wife because I was still in the hospital...

It came to a point where we were able to bury my wife ... on the 12th June... That night, when the State of Emergency was declared ... the security police stopped the night vigil. Then they said they only want people who were on their list... The security police took those people... When we were supposed to go to the graveyard, they came with an order that not more than 200 people should attend a funeral... People who were there were over 6 000 ... they came with horses, motor bikes and vans...

I opened a docket in Brits. I tried many times to make a follow up, people like [Fankie] Pretorius [a policeman], he would ask me – how's your leg? ... but to no avail... Their intention was to kill my entire family ... people were against forced removal and those who used the petrol bomb would be the state and nobody else.

Mr Meiring [TRC Commissioner]: What does one say to somebody, who's not only lost his property, but who lost his wife, whose children had to grow up without their mother? How can we compensate for that? We cannot... I marvel at the way at which you are not bitter and that you are willing to work for the community. You are the mayor now...[77]

Modimoeng was correct that an agent of the state had thrown the bomb, as Machiel (Fankie) Pretorius testified to the TRC. A member of the South African Security Police at the Brits sub-branch, he described how he had worked under the command of Robert Jubber. He and the other TRC applicants were supporters of the National Party; they saw it "as their duty to protect the government and defend it against what they saw as a revolutionary onslaught".[78] Pretorius deployed informers in political organisations and he evaluated the reports he received from his informers. He also intercepted correspondence and monitored activists' movements. All reports were submitted to Brigadier Jack Cronje, the commanding officer of the Northern Transvaal Security Branch Offices.

Pretorius believed that the BAC campaign had caused economic decline in Brits as a number of industrialists had left the area. He also believed that Oukasie residents should move to Lethlabile because of the chaos, lawlessness and anarchy caused by activists in Oukasie who intimidated residents not to move through the torching of administration buildings, houses, shops and vehicles, beatings, stonings, petrol-bombing and erecting barricades.

He was first instructed by Jubber to identify Sello Ramakobye's house because he "was an executive committee member of the BAC and wielded immense influence and political power in the community in general... The youth carried out orders from Leonard Brown who worked closely with Ramakobye and the leadership of the BAC." He met Lt Jacques Hechter and others in a dark parking lot, and instructed him to keep all activities a secret. They travelled to Brits in a minibus; when they arrived in Oukasie they put on balaclavas. He

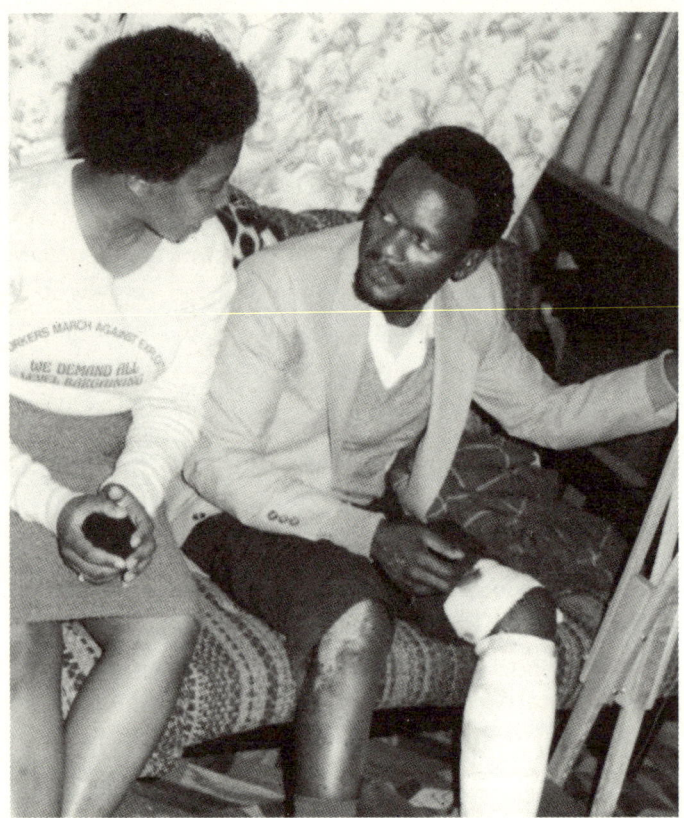

YCW member and MAWU organiser David Modimoeng recuperating from burns to his leg received during a petrol bomb attack on his house in Oukasie (Photo: B Fanaroff)

identified the houses and in the case of Brown he knew where his bedroom lay as "he had once conducted a search in the premises". On both occasions he waited at a distance watching petrol bombs being thrown. "After a while they returned speedily, they climbed back into the vehicle and we departed in haste. Just after we had departed, I heard a loud blow occurring behind me… As far as I know, nobody was injured or killed during these incidents."

The attack on David Modimoeng's house took a similar pattern. Pretorius testified:

> Modimeng [*sic*] was not only a prominent trade unionist but also a high-profile figure and participated in the affairs of the BAC. His wife, Joyce Modimeng [*sic*], also took part in the BAC and she was a well-known figure in [the] women's organisation in Oukasie and the anti-removal campaigns. There was also information that Modimoeng frequently travelled to Swaziland and Lesotho where he consulted with ANC members. The ANC members were said to be using him to smuggle weapons into the country.

After pointing out Modimoeng's house, Pretorius recalls:

> After a short while … Lt Hechter and another person came running past us in great haste and we returned with them to the vehicle, the white Nissan Skyline… Just after we departed, I heard a tremendous blow from the direction of Oukasie… The following morning upon my arrival at the office, I was informed by my colleagues that there had been an explosion at the residence of David Modimeng [*sic*] and that a person had died during the explosion, namely the spouse of Mr Modimeng [*sic*]…

During the TRC proceedings a legal representative for the Modimoeng family contradicted Pretorius's evidence that Modimoeng was an arms courier for the ANC and that his wife was a member of a women's organisation. In fact, she was a housewife with little interest in politics. It is difficult to know whether Pretorius or his informants were lying.[79] Jacobus van Vuuren and Jacques Hechter, of the security police, also testified to their role in the bombings but had a hazy recollection of events, as they had been involved in more than 300 other incidents. They accepted Pretorius's version of events. They were not local security police so had no personal knowledge of the people under attack. They worked as a team with the notorious Joe Mamasela, an *askari** in many illegal operations.[80]

There was a national and international outcry following Joyce's death. The Northern Transvaal Region of the Congress of South African Trade Unions (COSATU) boycotted white businesses and work canteens for two weeks. Such high-profile activists as Cyril Ramaphosa of the National Union of Mineworkers (NUM), COSATU president Elijah Barayi and Beyers Naude, founder of the banned Christian Institute of Southern Africa and dissident priest of the Dutch Reformed Church, came to Oukasie to show solidarity.

Jacob Moatshe commented, "It was too political for some people, and some residents moved to Lethlabile." The community showed bravery and restraint at Joyce's funeral, surrounded as they were by armed police and security vehicles. Moatshe observed:

> In the YCW we were disciplined and did not fight the police for the sake of fighting them [in contrast to the UDF's style of operation]. The YCW was a good cover. J.M. [Jean-Marie Dumortier] discouraged us from

---

* *Askaris* were former ANC operatives turned by the state to work for them. They were used to identify, kidnap or assassinate former comrades.

fighting the police. He'd say, 'The struggle is not a game with the police. It is a system.' He showed us not to fight the wrong enemy. Even at Joyce's funeral the police came, aiming their guns, and there could have been a massacre.

Immediately after the funeral, BAC members disappeared. They were in hiding or had been detained under Emergency regulations. Two major waves of detention without trial seriously affected the anti-removal mobilisation by BAC activists between 1986 and 1988. Yet these periods of forced exclusion from daily life were times of deep political discussion and learning for these activists. "Being at hiding provided a space for more political education. We learned from one another. A lot of political literature was circulated at such places and most comrades sharpened their political skills..." [81] The bonds

Mourners make their way to the graveyard, encircled by hundreds of police, at the funeral of Joyce Modimoeng, killed when her family house was firebombed. (Photo: B. Fanaroff)

between people in Oukasie were evident, as people took considerable risks to hide activists who moved regularly from place to place, seldom sleeping in the same place twice:

> Mary Mpete's house became a common meeting place and a safe hideout. We named her place 3 Step because of the number of steps you had to climb... She was a strong, stubborn and fearless mother who was prepared to lay down her life for us. Her fluency in Afrikaans gave her an advantage of communication and defending herself against the notorious Special Branch...
>
> Blacky Monare's place was strategically placed along the main road. This helped because many times police would pass without noticing or suspecting that we were hiding there... If walls could speak, Johanna Tele's place has a lot of history to tell... This was one of the bases for political school. Strategising, meeting and reception of foreign visitors was held here.[82]

Fourth stage of removal: Oukasie disestablished and services downgraded

Suddenly in October 1986, without warning, the government "disestablished" Oukasie.* Chris Heunis argued that "the astronomic cost involved in upgrading the town did not make its continued use a viable proposition". It would be upgraded for whites as soon as black people moved out.[83]

---

* To be disestablished meant that the Oukasie informal settlement would no longer officially exist. The few services that were provided by the state, such as the provision of water to communal taps, were withdrawn. The state's intention was to force people to move out of the settlement.

With the help of MAWU, NAAWU and TRAC, the BAC leadership had previously commissioned a feasibility study which estimated that R3 million would be needed to upgrade Oukasie. Now residents responded with an improvement plan by engineers and social scientists. According to that plan, an outlay of R1 115 000 would double water taps, upgrade storm drains, permit 10 communal flush toilets and grade roads. Another R1 911 000 would deliver water to each household, extend sewerage to each plot and tar two primary roads. Minister Heunis was not interested.[84]

At a meeting addressed by David Modimoeng, the community voted to stay away from work on 22 October 1986 to protest. Meanwhile the Black Sash mobilised national and international support. According to Alan Morris:

> Publicity is what TRAC is all about. During the 1960s and 1970s hundreds of thousands of people were moved without anyone knowing. It wasn't documented. The government hates publicity. Our weaponry is pretty limited: publicity, foreign pressure, trade union pressure and community pressure.[85]

The European Union, churches, political groups and students condemned the disestablishment of Oukasie and the *New York Times* carried articles on the intended removal.

At the beginning of 1987 the state demolished over a hundred homes, turned off the water, prohibited burials, stopped public transport, closed Itumeleng Primary School and the state crèche accommodating 200 children and transferred teachers to Lethlabile. The BAC responded

Community crèche after Brits was disestablished and the old crèche closed down (Photo: G. de Vlieg)

by encouraging the community to launch its own crèche. The community was in a state of great anxiety. Caroline Mashike remembers that after "the municipality closed off the water we went to the Roman Catholics and took cans on our heads to get water and we queued for water in the middle of the night." The process of downgrading community services was in full swing.

By now the Nationalists were turning somersaults in an attempt to reconcile reform with relocations in order to avoid the unwelcome international attention Oukasie's removal was bringing. In January 1988 Chris Heunis made the Transvaal Provincial Authority (TPA) responsible for moving "squatters" out of Oukasie. A month later, in February 1988, seventeen Oukasie community leaders were detained without trial.

PFP leader Helen Suzman denounced Heunis in Parliament for his insistence on removing the people of Oukasie. On 26 April 1988 Oukasie was declared an emergency camp for homeless people by Transvaal Administrator Willem Cruywagen in terms of the Prevention of Illegal Squatting Act. The entrance to the township was blocked and houses searched for squatters. At the same time, government raised rents by 80%.

The disestablishment did little to satisfy the white electorate, and the National Party lost its Brits seat to the CP in the May 1988 election. For Andrew Gerber, the Brits CP Member of Parliament, Oukasie remained a nasty "eyesore".[86]

In December 1988 Joseph Makama and three others who had lived in Oukasie sued Cruywagen in an attempt to invalidate the declaration of the emergency camp. In August 1989 advocate Arthur Chaskalson, the director of the Legal Resources Centre, represented the applicants.* In a surprise judgment, the conservative Justice Kees van Dijkhorst set aside the emergency camp ruling stating, "They can truly be called homes ... to their inhabitants... It follows that the decision of the respondent was substantially for an ulterior purpose and hereby rendered invalid."[87]

Over 2 000 people in Oukasie celebrated victory that night. The government's legal defeat, however, meant that the Conservative Party doubled its majority over the NP in the Brits municipality in September that year. The battle was not yet over.

---

* In 1994 Chaskalson became the first president of the Constitutional Court and Chief Justice of post-apartheid South Africa.

THREE

The Backlash

THE BOMBING OF THE Oukasie activists' houses in 1986 was the beginning of a new phase in the removal struggle. Up to this point the BAC had waged a disciplined battle with strict accountability to the community through mandating and report-back meetings.

Following the bombings some residents moved to Lethlabile and other locations out of fear, but most residents were not intimidated. For the state this meant that they had to find new tactics to force people out of Oukasie. There was a wave of detentions of BAC leadership in both 1986 and 1988, but this did not undermine the community's determination to remain in the township. The white right wing in Brits remained equally determined. After its victory on the Brits council in 1988, the Conservative Party (CP) quickly made it clear that removing Oukasie was not negotiable. The National Party (NP) at provincial and national levels was also not willing to concede. It would be too humiliating for them to yield. Instead, they developed a new and more insidious strategy.

This chapter looks at how this strategy unfolded in the late 1980s and the devastating impact it had on accountable organisation in Oukasie. The community was deeply divided by different factions. Their resort to violence created a climate of fear, which resulted in residents withdrawing from organised resistance.

Destroying organised resistance in Oukasie

Jean-Marie Dumortier remembers the joy when the first group of Oukasie activists were released from detention:

> [I heard] ululations in groups across the township, and liberation songs were ignited like little fires here and there. A young man told me, 'The location is celebrating this evening; it's welcoming its heroes.

He quickly qualified his joy by stating that it heralded the entrance to

> ... the valley of shadows where uncertainty, doubts and death reigned... Nothing was the same after that for the inhabitants of the old location. Instead of the frank struggle and solidarity ... came a troubled period which ate away at the unity and faith which had galvanised and brought residents this far.[88]

While the BAC leaders were in detention, a provisional committee – the Oukasie Residents Committee – had been set up to deal with administrative details such as donations for legal fees and for setting up a new crèche. According to Dumortier, "The merger of the old and provisional committees when the detainees returned was not easy."[89] At a meeting to celebrate their release, attended by various foreign embassies and churches affiliated to the South African Council of Churches (SACC),[*] Leonard Brown[90] gave a radical speech which "exasperated the old activists". He had been detained at the same time as the BAC leaders and "had problems co-existing with the others."[91]

During the research for this book, many people said that they believed that Leonard Brown had been "turned" by the police while in prison, and that he was now working as a state informer. Brown had once been an active, productive member of the BAC, and had been a target of state intimidation when his parents' house was firebombed in 1986. His comrades were greatly puzzled by his divisive, non-cooperative and violent behaviour after he was released from prison. A number of the people interviewed said that they suspected he was now collaborating with the state because that was the only way they could explain his changed behaviour. They alleged that he targeted committed activists in Oukasie. Dumortier recalls:

> With great skill he exploited the grievances that had come to light in the community, and most of all touched on the sensitive issue of money given to the previous committee which ... had never provided financial accounting to the residents despite their demands.[92]

Brown made allegations against the previous committee,

---

[*] The SACC was a prominent interdenominational Christian church organisation, under the leadership of general secretary Brigalia Bam, which opposed apartheid.

sowing doubt and division, which was spread by a young militant group he collected around him called "The Comrades". According to Jacob Moatshe, "The Comrades beat people, held people to ransom and demanded protection fees. Some people fled to Lethlabile".[93] At a BAC general meeting to vote in a new committee, the old leaders were "stung by the criticism" and did not stand for election. Brown packed the hall with some 200 of his supporters, and his followers were elected onto the committee.[94]

Brown then began attacking his opponents. Dumortier commented, "I came to see him as a psychopath who was excited by the extreme tension we were living in and was willing to do anything to seize power..."[95] Jacob Moatshe commented, "Popo Molefe [later premier of the North West Province] knew all about him. He called Brown 'Katsi' as he walked very softly from behind and surprised you." The shebeens of Oukasie, known for their high alcohol consumption, became the site of heated arguments; on a number of occasions members of the old BAC were stabbed and hospitalised after fights broke out. In the past, shebeens had been meeting places, information centres and sanctuaries. "There was no newspaper in Oukasie; the shebeen has the latest headlines," commented Richard Stengel.[96] Such vicious fighting was uncommon in the township. The police did not investigate these attacks, and residents began to feel that they were being delivered into a lawless reign of terror.

Over time Oukasie lost its vibrancy, as people were afraid to hold meetings or attend celebrations, and its alleyways went quiet. This eerie atmosphere was broken in March 1989. After a disagreement with Brown, another drinker took refuge in the house of Marshall Buys, former chairperson of the BAC, which was next to the shebeen. Brown and his followers besieged the house. In terror, the occupants barricaded the windows by pushing furniture against them, but they could not repulse the attackers. Buys went out and called on the attackers to be reasonable, but he was struck down by blows from clubs and hatchets, and then shot dead.

Marshall Buys, an early chairperson of the Brits Action Committee, later murdered (Photo: G. de Vlieg)

Leonard Brown was arrested but soon released on R1 000 bail. This shocked the community, which was traumatised by the slaughter. They saw Brown strolling around the streets accompanied by his Comrade bodyguards.[97]

Dumortier believed that during this time Oukasie residents were only held together by the churches and their priests and pastors. It was only in this way that people could meet and continue to make demands on the authorities. Former Firestone head shop steward Sello Ramakobye explained: "We had started many organisations so they could not target us so easily – youth, women, church organisations. Every month we held meetings at a different church."[98] On different occasions Moatshe and Dumortier visited Father Smangaliso Mkhatshwa of the Southern African Catholic Bishops Conference (SACBC) to appeal for help in dealing with the violence in Oukasie. Mkhatshwa was a well-respected activist who had been detained and house-arrested. He was also a patron of the United Democratic Front (UDF).[*] Mkhatshwa responded by helping to set up a Commission of Enquiry conducted by lawyers sponsored by the Defence of the Rights of Man (an international federation for human rights, based in Paris, France). The Commission visited the township and collected testimonies and documents from residents to pursue court cases. A measure of calm returned.

The violence that hit Oukasie was very similar to the generally tense environment in townships across the country which had brought Natal and the East Rand to the point of civil war in the late 1980s and early 1990s. Brown's behaviour became more erratic and threatening. Dumortier recalls him arriving in Oukasie once with a group of youth from Pretoria, and on another occasion with a group of Zulu men carrying machetes and traditional weapons. Brits and its surrounds, however, were affected by violence in a unique way.

---

[*] In 1996 Mkhatshwa became the Deputy Minister of Education, a post he held until 1999. He was elected to the ANC National Executive Committee in 1997. In 2000 he became the Mayor of the City of Tshwane (Pretoria).

Lethlabile's *askaris* – murderers, provocateurs and victims

As previously mentioned, Oukasie was notable for its lack of UDF and Umkhonto we Sizwe (MK) activity. Politics and community organisation were dominated by trade unionists and YCW activists. Despite the discipline shown by these organisations, in some respects this would work against the community.

From 1987 onwards, the state began to house *askaris* in Lethlabile, particularly in Zones 2 and 10, and in Hartebeesfontein. The state believed that by housing them in the Brits area they were less likely to be recognised by former ANC comrades and could keep their cover. *Askaris* themselves were terrified of reprisals should they be identified by activists or other MK members who had been infiltrated into the country. Sello Selepe, a former trade unionist and Oukasie resident, remarked:

> *Askaris* found an area where they could defend themselves against MK in their own township. They were heavy drinkers and would talk and identify themselves when drunk.* Joe Mamasela [a notorious *askari* who killed over forty activists[99]] lived in Zone 2 in Lethlabile. He sometimes came to our meetings in Oukasie. *Askaris* who came to Oukasie pretended to be comrades fleeing from Alex [Alexandra township in Johannesburg], and told us how they dealt with informants, and they urged us to do the same and also to stone delivery vans when

---

* Jacob Moatshe points out that *askaris* used the loose talk in shebeens to gather information and identify activists. This lifestyle inevitably meant that they became heavy drinkers themselves.

there were UDF consumer boycotts... They were agents provocateurs.[100]

Some of these *askaris* operated out of Vlakplaas, 48 kilometres from Brits. This was a farm where many executions of political opponents of the apartheid regime took place and where *askaris* were trained. Almond Nofomela was a venomous *askari* and hit-squad member who murdered many apartheid activists. He worked out of Vlakplaas but went for rest periods to Skeerpoort about 10 kilometres from Brits; he originally came from Bokfontein adjacent to Brits.[101]

Some *askaris* tried to give information to their former ANC comrades but with disastrous consequences. Brian Ngqulunga, an *askari* stationed at Security Branch headquarters in Pretoria, was murdered by his security police colleagues near Brits in July 1990 after he started providing names of *askaris*, operatives and informers to the ANC. He was dragged from his car and kidnapped by people in balaclavas. Thinking he was being attacked by MK, he shouted, "No, comrades, I am one of you!" He was taken to a deserted road near Lethlabile where a Captain Bellingham fired an entire magazine of AK47 bullets into his body.[102]

Hlokoza Motau believes that Lethlabile's *askaris* were used to assist in fomenting violence on the East Rand:

> We would see combis every morning going out to fetch them. A [Brits] NUMSA woman administrator told one of our regional office bearers [on the East Rand] that *askaris* wanted to get information on NUMSA people. She was friendly with them. She confessed and told us. She warned the office bearers.[103]

Jacob Moatshe remembers that "[Chris] Hani called them 'the most dangerous people in the country'. He knew them; some of them had been in his command."*

Peter Magagula, a Brits trade unionist who lived in Lethlabile, remembers being part of a campaign to expel *askaris* from the township:

> *Askaris* were not there when I first moved [to Lethlabile] in about 1985 or '86. We had three marches against their presence in early 1989. We demanded they be removed as they openly threatened people in leadership positions. Government was clandestinely involved with *askaris* ... and police [police lived on either side of him] said *askaris* were brought by the state into Lethlabile.[104]

Solly Phetoe was a regional secretary of the Congress of South African Trade Unions (COSATU) in the North West Province. He lived in Hartebeesfontein and worked for TRAC at the time of this story. He recalls that the state had brought some Koevoet members to live in Lethlabile and to train rural police. Koevoet was part of South African Battalion 31 which invaded Angola; it was known for its brutality and use of torture. When Namibia won its independence in 1989, Koevoet was disbanded and some of its members returned to South Africa to work for the apartheid government. [105]

Many activists were convinced that actor, playwright and former BAC executive member Abel Molokoane was shot and killed by agents of the state on the road from Oukasie to Lethlabile. Molokoane had witnessed the

---

* Chris Hani was a leader of the South African Communist Party and chief of staff of MK. He was assassinated in 1993.

slaughter of Marshall Buys and had announced afterwards:

> I know there are many of us who live in fear. A snake has slid into our community and sown hatred and death. We know him. I'm not afraid of accusing him publicly. Even if I have to give my life, I will give evidence in the trial. I will say what I know and he will be condemned.[106]

On 7 June 1990 Molokoane did indeed give his life. Eight days after the start of the trial, his body was discovered in the veld by the side of the road; his car was never found. Peter Magagula speculated, "*Askaris* killed him; nobody else would have done it – there were no serial killers in Brits!" Hlokoza Motau added that he was killed out on the open road because "if he was killed in Oukasie it would have been a problem for them".

The day after Molokoane's murder, Brown and his gang held a noisy braai [barbecue] in Oukasie. The trial was adjourned indefinitely and Brown was freed on the grounds of insufficient evidence.[107] He left Oukasie and went to live in Damonsville about five kilometres away. Established by the government in 1988, this new township was meant to house the small coloured population of Oukasie, in line with the state's policy of separating racial groups. Formerly, coloured and African people had all lived together in Oukasie.

The Varksquad brings both justice and fear

Oukasie residents were left feeling more vulnerable than ever, and they faced the dilemma of whether to retaliate and provoke a bloodbath or to do nothing and witness further slaughter. In this gap emerged a group of young people who aimed to protect the old BAC leaders and bring justice to their township. The new group set themselves up in opposition to Brown's Comrades and became known as the Varksquad (Pig Squad). According to Jacob Moatshe, their name came from a comment made by Captain Jubber of the Brits Security Branch, who had said they were a filthy group that wanted to live in squalor like pigs.

Brown's group by now had established itself as a vigilante group that operated outside the law, despite some of its members sitting on the BAC executive. Tshidi Mangoathe, YCW member and later Madibeng mayor, remembered it like this:

> Oukasie people defeated the regime, as they could not move them, so they [the state] started to recruit members of BAC and others to become vigilantes. That's when Marshall Buys was murdered, who had bravely led the Brits Action Committee with wisdom. There was terrible fear as soldiers were also in the township and the Varksquad was running up and down.[108]

Despite wanting to protect the community and openly identifying with the banned ANC, the Varksquad became another source of fear for residents.[109] The YCW had a consultative way of operating, and the aim of the former Brits Youth Committee had been to improve life through street committees – patrolling Oukasie, cleaning refuse and creating makeshift parks decorated with used car parts and tyres. In sharp contrast, these young men of the Varksquad were armed, and their way of protecting the community often meant using violence. Former trade unionist Sello

Selepe, who was a member of the Varksquad, spoke about the group:

> My group of eight was highly mobilised. The leadership of BAC, Marshall Buys, went overseas and was in touch with the ANC and they told him youngsters could join... We had contact with the UDF at a later stage, mainly through the church and Moses Mayekiso of the AAC [Alexandra Action Committee] who used to visit us. We indirectly participated in UDF campaigns.
>
> We were feared by the system [apartheid government] and some members of the community... We were *gatvol* [fed up] of what was happening to the community... We were armed through our Alex contacts. We protected the township and its leadership and fought fire with fire. We were young and militant and we liked this edge. After the State of Emergency was declared, soldiers came into the township and we challenged them and some were shot. We knew the township and it was dark at night so soldiers could not get into the township. We were in control.

Trade unionist Sello Ramakobye remembers the Varksquad's involvement in the bombing of a bus that was en route to Firestone via Bapong, Oukasie and Lethlabile. The youth had planned a march and stayaway in Oukasie and people were instructed not to go to work. When the bus arrived in the township, these activists told people to disembark; they then petrol-bombed the bus and it burned out. Thereafter all buses were prevented from entering Oukasie, and the only transport was via minibus taxis. Sello Selepe again:

We fought with Leonard Brown and the police. No police came into Oukasie. Consumer boycotts were enforced by us. We burned *bakkies* [small pick-up trucks] and lorries and buses that the state provided free for people to go and look at Lethlabile. Every move the authorities made, we had a counter action. Some police were sympathetic to Oukasie and gave us information.

The group attacked the houses of black councillors and policemen living in Oukasie. Marshall Buys explained how he was unwittingly caught up in an attack:

A group of kids walked up the hill singing that a policeman's house was burning... The house was built of wood. It was going up in flames. I thought, man, you cannot leave a house burning ... so we tried to put out the fire. The policeman was driving around looking for culprits. When he saw me, he fired a bullet. He came back and put a gun to me. After a few minutes, a bunch of cars came. Captain Jubber ... said, 'Let's talk.' He said, 'Get in the car.' Feinky [*sic*] Pretorius was driving. It was about 8 pm. They took me to the mortuary. They said, 'We'd like to get a tyre for you. What is your size?' They took a 13-inch tyre.* We drove down to the Crocodile River. They asked me a lot of questions. They asked me who burned Razwinane's shop... They hit me several times. The tied my hands in front with a very long rope. They put the tire around my neck ... and they pulled the tire against my throat and said, 'Tell the truth.' They took a petrol container ... and put some in my mouth and poured some

---

* "Necklacing" was a way of killing collaborators in townships. A tyre was placed around the neck, doused with petrol and set alight.

on the tire. I thought, 'I'm going to die.'[110]

Buys pretended he was going to tell Jubber the truth, and called him aside. Buying time saved his life, as the police were called away to another site. They dropped him at the station, accusing him of arson. "The next day Jubber showed me the minutes from BAC meetings. He said he had more informers than he needed in Oukasie and advised me to move out of Oukasie before I got killed."[111] Fateful words.

Sello Sclepe also recalls the Varksquad engaging in mob justice. "We would investigate a crime, like rape or an informant paid by the police, and convene a meeting with victims and accused somewhere in the community, and we participated in violence if they were guilty."[112] Hlokoza Motau said, "It was very difficult, as we saw wrongs by our own comrades. They would do attacks and then claim our support. They wanted support at all costs."

The older YCW leadership, such as Motau, were sympathetic to the Varksquad's aims. However, they believed these youth needed to be reined in, demobilised and allowed to mature. Selepe recalls that these older leaders arranged for him and others to attend a Saturday school at the University of the Witwatersrand:

> We were enlightened. BAC made sure we were educated, and we were separated and sent to different tertiary institutions. They said, 'It's time for you guys to go to school; you have dislodged the counter-revolutionary forces.' I went to college in Kimberley to become a teacher and I joined SANSCO [South African National Student Congress] and the NECC [National Education Coordinating Council].

Children looking at an Oukasie councillor's burned home – probably the actions of the Varksquad (Photo: G. de Vlieg)

Entrenching the use of taxis in the township indirectly also prolonged the violence. In the early 1990s, and reaching its height between 1995 and 1996, Lethlabile, Jericho, Oukasie, Maboloka and other routes around Brits were plagued by taxi violence. Different taxi operatives competed for market share using drive-by shootings, firebomb ambushes and paid assassins who made little distinction between operators and passengers. Hlokoza Motau remarked, "The taxi violence spilled into this [Oukasie] violence."

Taxi violence

The taxi conflict became interlinked with political interest groups. In Brits a number of retired police officers including *askaris* – who also operated as professional hitmen in drive-by shootings – muscled in on taxi routes. A *Sunday Nation* investigation established that people who attacked taxi commuters in Mamelodi in 1993 were hired by the Brits-based Lethlabile Taxi Association (LTA), some of whose members were *askaris*.[113] Many *askaris* lost their paid status as informers after 1993, when a political settlement in South Africa became inevitable and they turned to the taxi industry to make a living.[114]

Not surprisingly, Leonard Brown entered the taxi business and owned a taxi combi, which some alleged was bought with BAC money donated for use by the community crèche.[115]

The taxi violence on the Brits/Pretoria routes rumbled on, and only ended in 2006 when the ANC closed taxi ranks in Brits, and the LTA and the Brits Long Distance Taxi Association merged to form the Letlhabile-Brits United Local and Long Distance Taxi Association (Lebulldta). IOL News reported:

> The rivalry that turned the Brits area into a war zone ... and divided residents who grew up together and in which many innocent people died – is over. The war saw the entire LTA executive – chairman Moses Mdaka, public relations officer Mike Mangena and secretary-general Lawrence Kopano – thrown into prison. Mdaka and Mangena are serving 20 years, while

> Kopano is serving multiple taxi violence-related sentences, which includes a life term.[116]
>
> Provincial MEC Jerry Thibedi, opening the Lebulldta offices in Lethlabile, noted:
>
> > A day would hardly pass by in the 1995–1996 period without headline news in newspapers, radio and television about the taxi violence involving members of the LTA. The rattling sound of AK 47 assault rifles, sometimes late into the night or at pre-dawn, was not unusual in this township. Members of taxi hit-squads were a common sight on our major routes linking Lethlabile to Brits, Erasmus, Mabopane, Ga-Rankuwa and Pretoria... Following talks about talks, dating back to 2005, which culminated in a referendum, members of both associations agreed that it was in the best interest of the taxi industry of Lethlabile and Brits to form one united taxi association.[117]

Tension in white Brits

This already over-heated pot was brought even closer to boiling by the tense atmosphere that prevailed in the white town of Brits.

Deep rifts existed between different Afrikaner groups. There was the CP/NP divide that was described in Chapter 2. But the early 1990s was also the heyday of the Afrikaner Weerstandsbeweging (AWB). The AWB was a paramilitary fascist group dedicated to the creation of an independent *Boerestaat* [Afrikaner state] in South Africa. Its leader, Eugene Terreblanche, was based in the right-wing farming town of Ventersdorp, 142 kilometres from Brits. There, in August 1991, the Battle of Ventersdorp unfolded as the AWB confronted police in front of the town hall where President F.W. de Klerk was speaking. Two AWB members were killed and thirteen others were injured in clashes.[118]

Violent activity intensified as the survival of the apartheid state became more threatened. Japie Steenkamp, one of two National Party members on the Brits town council, recalls:

> On the council with the CP [Conservative Party], I was public enemy number one, as I agreed with the National Party's decision to release Mandela… The CP people came to Brits Print to my partner and told him that the mayor will take business away from us if 'Steenkamp does not toe the line'. He just said, 'Go to hell', and we lost the business.[119]

But it was the AWB, not the CP, that threatened the lives of Steenkamp and his family:

> I used to take a torch and baton and walk around the house at night. My daughter was called 'Mrs Mandela Junior' at school. They didn't like what was happening in the country and I became a symbol. They spat at me as I walked past in the street. But after 1994 these people started suddenly treating me OK. Brits is a small community…

In Oukasie the escalation of violence, coupled with the

continued destruction of people's homes as they moved out, led to more people leaving the township. Sello Selepe remembers his mother desperately wanting to move after Marshall Buys's murder, and he had to actively persuade her to stay. Ultimately about half of the Oukasie population moved – about 7 000 people. The state had only partially realised its aim of dislodging highly mobilised residents through fear and the tactic of violence begetting violence. In the process, however, by 1990 the BAC had collapsed under the weight of parallel structures, suspicion and violent confrontation.

Moving towards peace

The churches in Oukasie were alarmed by community disintegration. They intervened to investigate the violence and to create forums for peace. Jean-Marie Dumortier believed that, "The churches had the moral standing to stop violence outside of politics ... and to try to bring to the surface all shadowy plots."[120] Following Marshall Buys's murder in 1990, the South African Council of Churches, on invitation from the YCW, led an investigation into the violence. The report released in April 1991 concluded that the police were deeply involved in dividing the community by encouraging, and possibly covertly instigating, vigilante violence. Jacob Moatshe recalls that the UDF Secretary for the Transvaal region, Popo Molefe, was particularly helpful in trying to resolve and calm the situation in Oukasie.

Then about three years after this explosion of violence in Oukasie, on 27 January 1991, Transvaal administrator Danie Hough announced that the Cabinet had decided that Oukasie would remain a residential area, that the residents could stay permanently and that it would be upgraded.

Richard Abel has commented that legal strategies played a vital role in preventing the government's exercise of unlimited power as "judicial decisions enjoyed considerable legitimacy". He argues that:

> Functional divisions between executive, legislature, and judicial branches and national and local government can lead to divergent attitudes. Personal differences between legislators, judges, even ministers can hobble action ... the state could not promote its reformist image and cultivate loyalty of Whites ... the law slowed the progress of grand apartheid until politics could reverse it.[121]

This is indeed true, but the law did not operate in a vacuum. It was but one weapon, albeit an important one, used by highly mobilised and organised residents who made use of all resources available to them. Their determination to stay in their homes, on their land among their ancestral graves, despite a reign of terror waged against them, whittled away the authority of the apartheid state. This was given added force by the undermining of state power in every township across the country, to even the most remote rural community.

It was only after Oukasie's reprieve that "things began to calm down in the location", as Peter Magagula stated.

The National Peace Accord signed in September 1991, which was a critical step towards political negotiations in South Africa, also began a long process of bringing peace to the country. Brits, a storm centre of forces fomenting violence, now had to embark on a process of bringing peace and reconstruction. The ANC turned its attention to finding a place in society for Lethlabile's *askaris*. Chris Hani was sent on a fact-finding mission by the ANC leadership.

Soon after that, Tokyo Sexwale, who had been an MK operative in the early 1970s, addressed the *askaris* in Lethlabile Stadium. The aim was partly an attempt to change their mindset and transform them so they could be integrated into society, and partly to persuade them to seek amnesty in any future national reconciliation process. The National Peace Accord addressed the future role of the police and introduced a range of structures and methods of operation which they would have to observe.[122] It also directly addressed the position of *askaris* whose services were terminated, and there was agreement that the NP government would pay them out. Peter Magagula noted that many still live in Lethlabile, but also that some had died owing to their loose lifestyle, and some had turned to crime and had been murdered or ended up in jail.

Ironically, the NP's elaborate social engineering plan, including its long battle to stamp out Oukasie, had spawned the only development available to black people around Brits. The township of Mothutlung, with its improved housing and infrastructure, grew out of a desire to move Oukasie residents. Likewise, Lethlabile and Damonsville were constructed in the 1980s and provided housing, water, electricity and water-borne sewerage to Brits's black population. It was only the long-suffering residents of Oukasie who had yet to enjoy any such development. As Antonio Gramsci describes, in major transition periods, "the crisis consists precisely in the fact that the old is dying and the new cannot be born; in this interregnum a great variety of morbid symptoms appear."[123] Oukasie's people had lived through the morbid symptoms and had not been crushed. It was now important to move forward.

FOUR

The People's Municipality: Oukasie Development Trust

A MONTH BEFORE Oukasie's reprieve, on 24 December 1990, the Young Christian Workers (YCW) held a year-end meeting. The hall was full. The last such meeting had been held in 1984 and thereafter the State of Emergency had ended all possibility of gathering openly. In the year of Nelson Mandela's release, a reawakening was taking place in Oukasie and people were tentatively emerging from a mantle of fear. Jean-Marie Dumortier remarked:

> They had lived years in a quasi-clandestine state in little groups... I was struck by the youth of the people present. The average age [in the YCW] in the early 1980s was closer to the thirties than twenties but today the youngsters were 17–18 years old. The atmosphere had lightened. No furtive glances to the exit to check for police cars or look at an unknown face that may be an informer. There were

plays, poems, trade union songs, to the glory of the South African people. Old activists were there who had all been the object of violence and detentions.[124]

In the calmer atmosphere that followed, in 1991 the United Democratic Front (UDF) mobilised the Oukasie leadership to set up a civic structure to replace the shattered Brits Action Committee. The well-supported Oukasie Civic Association (OCA) was launched, and Phineas Ngale was elected its chairperson. Ngale had grown up with Jacob Moatshe's family and was both a YCW activist and influential in the student movement. Sello Selepe commented, "After Abel [Molokoane] was killed and Chippa Mongalo was also killed, people dropped out of BAC, but the civic association brought in new, fresh, young leadership as a deliberate strategy."[125]

The OCA created the Oukasie People's Delegation (also known as Friends of Oukasie). According to Jacob Moatshe, this allowed outside advisors to participate in sub-structures to deal with health, education and welfare issues.[126] The OCA tentatively embarked on a development course. The township remained grindingly poor, with houses set among twisted alleyways that had no lighting and boasting only one main-access gravel road. The only service it received from the municipality was the collection of night-soil buckets placed outside people's doorways. Houses with toilets, electricity and clinics, schools, recreation facilities, public facilities such as a library and easy access to tap water were all unknown luxuries.

Taffy Adler was a former trade union organiser for the National Automobile and Allied Workers' Union (NAAWU). He believes that Brits's political leanings at the time had a decisive impact on the NP's decision to abandon the removal and to develop Oukasie:

> Coming out of the removals and the political dispensation that occurred as a result of Brits going Conservative was a decision by government [which implied] … 'Okay, white Brits, you've gone Conservative. Stuff you. We're now going to let the township stay.' It was as petulant as that. 'You guys want to fuck with us, we're now going to fuck with you … and we're going to develop it.'[127]

But how could Oukasie's residents influence government's development plans and move beyond the dislocation and violence that they had experienced? As Sello Selepe put it:

> After the reprieve, what to do? The municipal offices had been burned and councillors had been driven out – there was no municipal assistance left. We held a general meeting, I remember, with the Black Sash present, to begin the process of rebuilding.

This chapter charts the development of Oukasie in the wake of the State of Emergency and the violence which had shocked the community. The community owned the Oukasie Development Trust (ODT), which was the instrument of this development; the work itself was mainly completed in the early 1990s in the run-up to South Africa's first democratic elections. YCW members and trade unionists were an important part of this initiative, although they now wore different hats.

Building the Oukasie Development Trust

In 1991 the Transvaal Provincial Authority (TPA) began a planning process in Oukasie to deliver infrastructure to its 14 000 residents. It did this through the Independent Development Trust (IDT). The IDT was a relatively enlightened semi-government structure. It had been launched in 1990 to address the housing crisis in South Africa. It chose to deliver a site-and-service product, where it granted a subsidy to households in informal settlements whose applications were successful. Oukasie was such a settlement. Members of the Oukasie People's Delegation – such as Taffy Adler, Geoff Budlender from the Legal Resources Centre (LRC) and others who pledged solidarity – began to play a role in accessing subsidies and assisting the community to realise its development goals.

Lynn Pikholz, who studied the provision of informal housing in South Africa, later commented:

> I noticed that the residents of Oukasie managed to accomplish far more than other similar upgrades within the same timespan. Within just three years, from being 'illegal' and on the bucket sewage system, all households had their own water connection and toilet as well as access to a range of community facilities.[128]

Why was this?

Taffy Adler believes it was a combination of good luck, good leadership and good technical support. When he became involved, the TPA had begun a planning exercise led by Arnold Aap – a "paternalistic planner" in the provincial administration who "just wanted to help the blacks", according to Adler. Aap was interacting with the very people that the TPA had attempted to remove just six months before. The TPA appointed Pretoria-based engineering contractors Bouwer Viljoen as project managers.

Adler provided the organisational skills he had developed in the union, as did Michael Oelofse, an expert on housing from the Urban Foundation. The Foundation, an institution backed by the private sector, had been established in the wake of the 1976 Soweto Riots to improve the built environment of urban black people. It was viewed with suspicion by some activists because of its links with capital. These skills were complemented by those of Ulli Bleibaum and Otto Barnard who, according to Adler, were "the best technical people on site-and-service development". Adler went on to say:

> They didn't know what had hit them. They had never come across such articulate, organised, responsive people – people who had grown up with the unions and the YCW and had long interaction with people like Jean-Marie [Dumortier] from the Catholic Church, and the LRC and Black Sash – which allowed for a building of trust and for Oukasie leadership to be outward looking. There was a remarkable leadership cadre that makes Brits distinctive, with a long history of organisation in a highly political struggle.

The IDT insisted on community participation and would only finance the Oukasie development project on condition that it was set up as a community development trust. Initially this was viewed as an unfortunate delay but, as luck would have it, using the trust allowed the project to be completed in record time. While the project managers

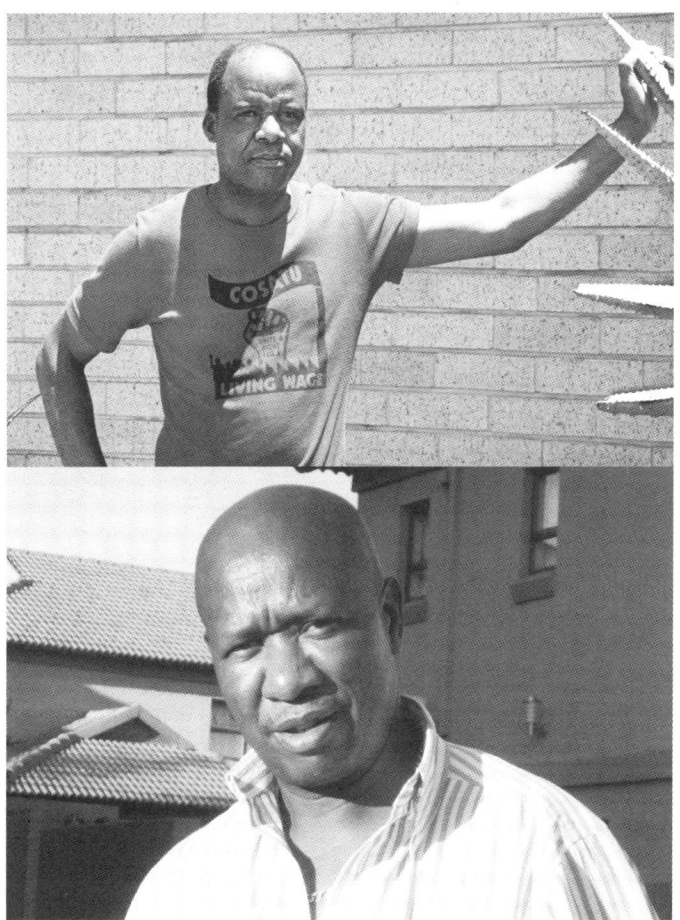

Levy Mamabolo and Jacob Moatshe were the kingpins of the Oukasie development project. (Photo Mamabolo: G. de Vlieg; Photo Moatshe: K. Forrest)

"scrambled" to get a trust in place, Taffy Adler recalls that Ulli Bleibaum and Otto Holicki engaged in an intensive community-based planning process for "months on end, going late into the night and came up with a good plan". The Oukasie Development Trust was inaugurated in March 1992 and fell under OCA as its development wing and financing arm.

Caroline Mashike was a Trust member. She had originally been drawn into the removal struggle by the BAC. Mashike recalls that, in the beginning, "We [ODT] had no offices. We used the Roman Catholic church offices. Everyone for the development project registered and paid 50 cents."[129] According to Adler, the "king-pins" were YCW's Jacob Moatshe, who was Community Liaison Officer (and later Chief Executive Officer), and Levy Mamabolo, NUMSA head shop steward at Robert Bosch, who was the political figure. He was "wise, patient highly respected – perfect for the job," said Adler, and he chaired the Trust's Board of Directors. Oelofse and Adler also sat on the Board, which appointed various sub-committees including the important technical committee. Moatshe was trained and given a salary for two years, during which time he worked tirelessly in building ODT sub-committees and helping people to access the resources they needed.

The ODT also strategically invited a National Party member onto its Board – Japie Steenkamp, a former councillor and owner of Brits Print. Steenkamp was now actively opposing the far right wing on the Brits council. According to Adler, "He played a constructive role. He would print for free – newsletters and so on – and as he was a businessman, he was constructive on the Trust." Steenkamp recalls:

It dawned on me that I was indoctrinated. The time has

passed for this. Let's accept Oukasie will never be moved. And CP [Conservative Party] councillors said to me, 'If you've lost your mind don't ask us to lose ours'... I decided I must get involved as a parallel thing to Council. We worked for four years together... Mamabolo was a wonderful Mandela-type figure... I used to go to Oukasie on Saturday mornings for ODT meetings, and my wife was in tears about my safety but I went and I said to her 'they are just ordinary people...'[130]

Church leaders such as Peter Moatshe from the South African Council of Churches (SACC), who had long supported the anti-removal struggle, also sat on the Board and provided continuity with the township's history.

Managing politics and finances

The ODT trustees were careful to work with the Civic Association, realising that there was the potential for a competitive relationship to develop as the OCA's prime aim was to provide development for residents. Civic Association leaders sat on the Trust (Eliot Mayisela and Phineas Ngale initially), and regular discussions occurred between the leadership of the two groups. This proved to be especially important when new OCA leadership was elected. The ODT, learning from the implosion of the BAC, also emphasised the importance of managing conflict. So, for example, when the Civic Association complained it was under-resourced, the ODT offered to share its offices and equipment, and this regular contact assisted in containing rumours and suspicion. They agreed on clear roles – the Civic Association would liaise with the community on all upgrading issues at mass meetings, and the ODT would be responsible for consolidating land and upgrading infrastructure through the work of its technical sub-committee. In consequence, both structures were respected by the community and both benefitted from the project.[131]

The ODT's transparent way of working meant that it was able to use regular community meetings to create trust and to share problems and responsibility. The organisation's consultants explained technical information at meetings. By doing so, they increased the community's knowledge and ownership of the project, lowered costs and allowed people to speak with authority when negotiating with different actors. The Trust, showing the influence of the unionists on its Board, developed a dispute resolution policy which was particularly important in site allocation and border disputes. In cases of dispute, a formal committee convened. If the grievance was resolved, all parties signed an agreement. However, if it was not resolved, a mediator was appointed who was respected by both parties.[132]

The ODT hired technicians, and Otto Holicki – who worked in Oukasie at least three days a week – checked the quality of the work and implemented control mechanisms to ensure that the agreed plan was implemented. Taffy Adler observed, "There was substantial organisation, genuine political leadership and serious professionalism, which allowed for good, serious development." Geoff Budlender set up the Trust's constitution and a Brits firm of accountants was employed to oversee all financial matters. Adler believes that Jacob Moatshe's style of leadership was critical: "Jacob was confident enough to handle external support and had no problem about employing accountants, auditors and so on."

The project was also free of corruption. Japie Steenkamp recalls: "I insisted on auditing the ODT... We always had a clean audit and we handled millions of rand." Moatshe also remarked, "I don't mess with community funds. I hate corruption. We appointed auditors from the inception of the project and we never got a negative audit." Wherever possible, the project used local labour which was motivated to work speedily, and Moatshe leaned on the TPA to rapidly draw down finances so these small contractors could be paid to continue their work. Trust members gave freely of their spare time and were continuously available to solve difficult problems, such as when squatters invaded land allocated for housing. They were also on tap to negotiate with state departments where necessary.

Oukasie's success was in part due to its politicised leadership, who used political tactics and connections to achieve the Trust's goals. For example, when a destructive group in the local ANC began badmouthing certain trustees, it called in respected ANC leadership to diffuse the jealousies. A TPA representative on the technical committee informed the ODT of unspent money available at the end of the year from the Regional Services Council budget, and the ODT was able to access this. And when the Department of Education persistently ignored the community's request for funds to build schools, residents threatened to stage a sit-in at its offices; the ODT also called in the media to publish photos of children learning in dilapidated classrooms. Lynn Pikholz observed that this ran "contrary to traditional advice that planners and policy makers usually give, namely that a successful upgrade depends on a separation of politics from technical aspects of a project".[133] Instead of ignoring politics, the ODT openly established mechanisms to deal with it and used the community's overwhelming support for the ANC to its advantage.

The Trust was also adept at raising finance and skilfully investing it, and its successful implementation made it an attractive project for donors. Funders such as USAID, Kagiso Trust and the Brits business community (particularly multinationals) were keen to support a well-managed and financially solid endeavour. Brits businesses tended to work through people such as Bert Badenhorst, chairperson of the Brits Industrial Association. The YCW's Hlokoza Motau remarked:

> Industry and police – we thought they had a connection. HR [human resources] managers, they used to meet to deal with security issues [during the removal struggle]. Most managers like this have now retired. But they were to be more helpful in this later [ODT] period.[134]

Even the CP town council eventually came on board and agreed to extend services to the township. They also agreed to finance high-mast lighting, which the community had surprisingly chosen over street lights. Japie Steenkamp recalls:

> When they discussed street lighting versus high-mast lighting, they preferred high mast. I was surprised. I learned a lot of things. Once at an ODT meeting people were saying, 'We don't feel safe'. So I said I would use my contacts with the police. They protested, 'Please don't bring in the police.' It was like a crackerjack under me the way they reacted, and later when I heard on the TRC what the police did I understood.

Delivering the goods

By the time of South Africa's first democratic elections in April 1994, every house in Oukasie had its own water connection and outside flush toilet, as well as access to community facilities including two primary schools, a maternity and health clinic, a sports and recreation field, roads, including a tarred main road into Oukasie, mail boxes, public phones, a community hall and a library.

The ODT had successfully assisted residents to access site-and-service subsidies while simultaneously negotiating with the Regional Services Council to electrify the township. The lights were first switched on in a memorable moment in 1994. A little later, in 1996, a shaded taxi rank was built in Oukasie and security was installed at the crèche and community hall to stop vandalism. The project had also created substantial employment. The first phase of Oukasie's development was over.

In 1995 Levy Mamabolo commented in the ODT's annual report:

> We have managed to transform [Oukasie] into a decent place that has become desirable to live in. So much so that some of the problems we have faced this year has been invasion of homeless people and the need to develop at least one extension to the township.[135]

The original IDT site-and-service grants provided for such an extension, and the ODT acquired new agricultural land in Oukasie and also created the new Oukasie North. The ODT obtained 600 subsidies from the National Housing Commission to provide housing in Oukasie

Electricity is turned on for the first time in Oukasie. (Photo: T. Adler)

North. By this time, Geoff Budlender was the director general of Land Affairs in the new ANC government. Together with Derek Hanekom, the Minister of Land Affairs, he helped to release land for further development, land which the ODT discovered was being held in a private trust. The ODT signed an agreement with the new Transitional Local Council (TLC) to develop the land, while the Trust continued to supervise. Levy Mamabolo commented that "delicate negotiations around the criteria for residence were carried out successfully". [136] Contractors continued to employ local labour and to maximise labour-intensive work such as digging trenches and laying pipes; they also conducted skills upgrading programmes.[137]

In 1995, 1 665 sites had been transferred and registered in the name of Oukasie owners. However, because much of democratic South Africa's legislation was still in the making, the process of transferring ownership to residents would plague the ODT for years to come. Levy Mamabolo's 1996 report noted, "285 sites sat in limbo because of the inability to register them as the Local Government Transition Act made it impossible."[138] The passing of the Land Administration Act in December 1995 finally allowed state land to be transferred to the local authority and to individuals, but the ODT was again frustrated when internal disagreements surfaced in the Department of Land Affairs. Taffy Adler commented:

> The land was government owned under the Republic of South Africa and to transfer it took a lot of effort and time in the bureaucratic deeds office. We needed to register the land for 750 houses, as it was an informal settlement. Jacob [Moatshe] was persistent while we were developing ... a lot of houses were built but transfer of land was difficult and local people needed to push for deeds transfer.

Both the 1996 and 1997 ODT Annual Reports also pointed out that the ODT was unable to access IDT subsidies to the tune of R3 367 million for 449 sites until the land ownership issue was resolved. (Transfer of the remaining land to the local authority was only achieved in 2002, and Oukasie only received full status as a residential area in 2005.)

In 1996 construction of new two-roomed houses began in Oukasie North despite labour disputes, rain delays and the necessity to move squatters. The ODT once again had successfully negotiated – this time with the National Housing Commission, the state's housing instrument

The Levy Mamabolo Community Hall in Oukasie (Photo: K. Forrest)

before new provinces were established – to finance the building of 600 houses on the serviced sites. Owing to the bad soil in the area, special housing foundations were designed to avoid cracks, and houses were built to allow for eventual expansion. By 1997, 200 houses were occupied and some owners were making improvements such as paving, tiling, erecting washing lines and adding on corrugated-iron room extensions. By 1998, owners could apply for water, sewerage and electricity connections.

The ODT had by this time formed an alliance with the South African Homeless People's Federation, an international organisation which focused on providing houses for squatters and shack dwellers. It was run by Abel Molokoane's sister, Rose. Although not a major player in the housing arena, it was a fruitful, if sometimes

The well-stocked and well-used library in Oukasie (Photo: K. Forrest)

competitive, partnership. The Homeless Federation was able to access further subsidies to build a number of houses on the serviced sites. In addition, in the post-1994 period, the municipality and Habitat for Humanity used the serviced sites to build houses, as did private individuals who managed to get loans.

Schooling and job creation

Through ongoing fundraising and wise investment, the Trust built up reserves of R20 million to continue operating after 1994 when many donors withdrew from South African development projects because they believed this was now the role of democratic local authorities.

Other communities around Brits had watched with

considerable interest as the ODT leveraged new housing and community facilities for Oukasie. The ODT was sensitive to local claims that only Oukasie benefitted from its development initiatives. Thus the second phase of development – which focused on education with a particular emphasis on science, technology and teacher upgrading – targeted both Oukasie and Greater Brits. Chief Executive Officer (CEO) Jacob Moatshe stated in his 1998 Annual Report:

> When we started ODT we focused narrowly on developing Oukasie. We then became more involved in facilitating development and extended our focus to Greater Brits by participating in regional business and technical upgrade schemes, and also worked with government agencies such as the Brits TLC.[139]

The ODT developed a relationship with a sister project in Berkeley, California, which assisted with upgrading science teachers at primary and high schools. In 1998 it employed a former University of the Witwatersrand director of the Science and Education Project (SEP) to steer its science programme with teachers. This resulted in the upgrading of teachers' skills in 66 primary schools in and around Oukasie. An ODT–SEP programme in 1999 provided practical lessons for teachers in the Greater Brits area and conducted 26 workshops attended by 2 000 science teachers. "Our learners achieved distinctions, and Jacob [Moatshe] gave some of his own money for bursaries," recalls ODT trustee Caroline Mashike. In 1999 a Science and Technology Centre was completed in Oukasie by local contractors (built within six months). It housed 20 computers and ran regular computer courses for the community.[140]

Less successful was the ODT's attempt at job creation and the stimulation of entrepreneurial activities, although between 1997 and 2000 it had some small success.

In the early 1980s attempts had been made to assist Oukasie residents to develop sewing, fencing and brickmaking cooperatives, all of which had failed. There were several reasons for this: they did not generate sufficient surplus to pay members regularly, members were largely untrained in small business skills, economies of scale meant that the sewing co-op could not compete with larger suppliers and lack of start-up capital meant the brickmaking initiative was stillborn and high transport costs to purchase raw materials were unsustainable.[141] Now the ODT attempted to enter the job creation arena by making loan capital available and by ensuring accessible training.

The ODT put considerable effort into the Greater Brits Investment Group (GBIG), a sub-committee of the Greater Brits Development Forum. It worked with industrialists, business people and trade unions to develop a vehicle to stimulate economic activity in Greater Brits. The IDT committed funding for three years and a Trust was established. The YCW's Sam Mkhabela and Jacob Moatshe represented the ODT on its Board. Two lead projects were identified – sand mining and sawdust recycling for the manufacture of briquettes.

The GBIG purchased land 10 kilometres from Brits and the sand mined was sold as plaster sand, top soil and filling. The venture created jobs for 10 people. The GBIG received a royalty on sales, which was reinvested. It also fundraised R2.8 million for job creation projects. It assisted entrepreneurs with small business plans in areas like tyre repairs, computer training, general dealing and chicken farming. By 1999 the GBIG had created 65 jobs and facilitated wealth creation in small and medium enterprises to the tune of R4.2 million and secured R9.6 million for new investment in SMMEs.

Ultimately, however, the ODT was unable to obtain sufficient financial and other support from local industry, and the new municipality and district council showed little inclination to support the initiative. Most of the small businesses collapsed.[142]

The rise of the ANC and the decline of the white right

In the early 1990s the ODT worked dedicatedly to implement development in the absence of effective municipal structures. At the same time, the newly unbanned ANC began to build its structures to prepare for the taking of power and the first national democratic elections. Brits was no exception. The town transformed into an excited buzz of new organisations and activities.

Brits's first overarching ANC branch was launched in 1992 at the Primindia Community Hall, and among its members were many former YCW and union activists. They came from a wide area including Mothutlung, Maboloka, Oukasie, Primindia, Segwaelane, Bapong and Majakaneng. The branch's first organiser and political education officer was Eliot Mayisela, who had earlier been expelled from the YCW because of his individualistic and populist approach to politics. He organised Mandela's first visit to Brits, which was a success (despite AWB threats to assassinate Mandela). As a result, he was noticed by the ANC Gauteng regional leadership and was recruited as an ANC regional organiser.[143]

In 1993 a number of ANC branches were established in and around Brits, including in Oukasie. The Oukasie branch's first executive included Levy Mamabolo as Chairperson, Phineas Ngale as Deputy and Tshidi Mangoathe and Caroline Mashike as members. Leonard Brown was also elected onto the executive by his usual supporters, despite his alleged role in Marshall Buys's murder. A branch of the South African Communist Party (SACP) was also launched. Its leadership included Levy Mamabolo, Tshidi Mangoathe, Sello Selepe, Wanda Makgale from the Oukasie women's organisation and Jerry Morulane and Cyprian Phasha from NUMSA.

Running parallel to these new organisational initiatives was the continued presence of the Brits Council, dominated by the Conservative Party (CP). It was financially very stable, according to Bert Botha:

> [It was] the richest in the whole of the Transvaal because of our mining, farming, manufacturing. We rented land out and the farming community did well. This was before the decline of the tobacco industry. Platinum was big. Bridgestone, ATC – the biggest South African companies were in Brits. We taxed manufacturing heavily. We had so much money that the financial manager of the council had to be reprimanded for taking interest and reinvesting it, which was against the law.[144]

The CP built new municipal offices and refurbished the City Hall. It built sewerage and water purifying plants using water from the Crocodile River, a country club, roads, a service centre for old people consisting of a hall surrounded by houses and a covered taxi rank where people could sell their wares. But despite its wealth, it did not develop any of the surrounding townships or villages.

The CP kept a stranglehold over the council. Dr Botha recalls, "We were totally opposed to the Nats [National Party members] and we kept them out of all decisions." Japie Steenkamp experienced it from the other side:

> We Nats fought tooth and nail. The CP were political dreamers, never realistic, and never got realistic. The CP wanted to make Andries Treurnicht [the CP leader] an honorary Brits citizen. I walked out of the council but they did it.

While the CP spent lavishly, a parallel structure was being created. The National Party (NP) instructed each town council to set up small consultative CODESA-like structures to pave the way for a local transition to democracy.*

In 1993 the government passed the Local Government Transition Act in order to promote the restructuring of local government and to allow for the establishment of forums to negotiate such restructuring. The Act also allowed for the election of interim transitional councils and for the establishment of Local Government Demarcation Boards.

The CP in Brits, still resisting change, refused to establish these structures. Meanwhile Bert Badenhorst, who was head of human resources at Robert Bosch, was under

---

* The Convention for a Democratic South Africa (CODESA) was the national body conducting political negotiations for a transition to democracy in South Africa.

pressure from its German parent company on the question of head shop steward Levy Mamabolo's detention. This, combined with the CP's stubbornness, led Badenhorst and Japie Steenkamp to establish the Brits Coordinating Committee because, according to Badenhorst, "We saw the CP council was very negative for business." [145] They started to talk to trade unions and the South African National Civic Organisation (SANCO), and managed to get some people released from detention. "The CP refused to give the city council hall for meetings so we met at the fire station and brought our own chairs," recalls Badenhorst.

Badenhorst also remembers a meeting where the Afrikaner Weerstandsbeweging (AWB) arrived fully uniformed and armed with rifles. Members of the National Union of Metalworkers of South Africa (NUMSA), the Congress of South African Trade Unions (COSATU), the South African National Civic Organisation and the Brits Sakekamer (Afrikaans business chamber), as well as industrialists, were sitting tensely inside. Negotiations ensued with AWB leaders, and representatives from the meeting stressed to them that anyone was permitted to participate. Finally the AWB agreed to leave their weapons outside and enter. They announced they wanted Brits to become a *Boerestaat* – an independent Afrikaner state – and threatened to block roads and highways to protest political negotiations. At the meeting, industrialists expressed concern that multinational companies would leave Brits. Badenhorst, who saw that "the CP council now felt left out", invited it to a subsequent meeting to talk about the withdrawal of capital:

> At the meeting Nicholas de Jager, the CP mayor, stood up

and said, 'When there is a *Boerestaat* we will be in power. Unions will be banned and business will flourish.' I pointed out that banning unions might result in the withdrawal of international companies. 'Let them withdraw,' he said, 'we will do the manufacturing without blacks.' There were many confrontations and uncertainties – the industrial situation was very unstable.

Although the CODESA-like negotiating forum in Brits was never promoted by the CP council, the alternative Coordinating Committee probably played an important role in diffusing tensions in a profoundly polarised town. By the time the Transitional Local Council was established, people of varying political persuasions had confronted and at least listened to each other.

The ANC won a majority in the April 1994 elections and formed South Africa's first democratic government. But after all its sound and fury, what happened to Brits's CP and NP members? According to Steenkamp, "People in Brits accepted a black government very quickly. South African whites just said, 'I'll stand to one side and won't get aggressive,' and Brits did well – we just go on with things." Steenkamp's worried mother asked what he thought of the new country and he answered, "Are my brothers and me any worse off?"

Dr Botha, former CP mayor, commented that after the ANC took power many CP members joined the Democratic Party (DP) and some lost interest in politics. A few crossed to the National Party, the African Christian Democratic Party (ACDP) and the Herstigte Nasionale Party (HNP). He stated, "White politics is non-existent. The old politics was all about black and white; it was not the right way to go... I think I wasted some time on politics."

A vision achieved

Oukasie residents began an important journey when they decided they were not going to be moved. This voyage had led them on a development path where the OCA, and more particularly the ODT, assumed the role of a municipality in the absence of democratic local government in South Africa. As Jacob Moatshe commented:

> The civic saw itself as a state substitute body performing functions not being done by the state. The civic felt responsible for providing schools, clinics, basic services. We refused to affiliate to the UDF or SANCO, as we were worried they would not focus.

Throughout this long journey, YCW and trade union leadership had stayed the course. They had worked closely with residents and had helped the community to realise its vision. In an extraordinary achievement, commented Taffy Adler, the ODT "had brought all the best elements of development together – schools, crèches, community upgrading – in a coincidence of luck and how to take advantage of it." Mobilisation, community activism and the transition from activism to development work had meshed with good leadership and professional expertise.

It was now the responsibility of Brits's new democratic local government to ensure that these services were maintained, and to take forward the further development needs of this growing community.

FIVE
A New Era and a Difficult Birth

FOLLOWING THE NATIONAL elections in April 1994, the people of Brits established a Transitional Local Council (TLC), which was mandatory under the 1996 Local Government Transitional Amendment Act. This interim phase of local government had to complete its work by the year 2000, at which time elections would be held to vote in councils for new demarcated municipalities.

The goal of this restructuring was to provide local authorities with greater autonomy within democratic principles in order to provide more effective service delivery. The people of Brits arrived in their numbers in 1995 to choose their new TLC. The election resulted in a majority of African National Congress (ANC) councillors being elected – ANC 16, Brits Rate Payers Association 6, National Party (NP) 3 – bringing it to a total of 25 councillors.[146]

This chapter examines the changing landscape that

the new ANC democracy brought to Oukasie. It follows Oukasie's leadership and its contribution to the Brits Transitional Council from 1995, and its eventual sidelining when a new leadership in the Madibeng municipality (which includes Brits, Oukasie and Lethlabile) ushered in a period of failed service delivery from 2000.

The Brits Transitional Council

Not surprisingly, some of the ANC councillors and Council officials that had been elected to the transitional council had roots in the Young Christian Workers (YCW), trade unions and the Oukasie Development Trust (ODT). David Mokase, a shop steward for the National Union of Metalworkers of South Africa (NUMSA), was elected, as was ODT's Caroline Mashike. A little later, in 1997, YCW's Tshidi Mangoathe became a councillor. NUMSA shop steward July Khoza and YCW and ODT chairperson Sam Mkhabela became Council officials. Former trade unionist Sello Selepe recalls that there was "huge commitment from NUMSA. NUMSA negotiated with Bosch to release people for work on the Council for 10 years, and then they could return to work."[147]

NUMSA shop steward and ODT chairperson Levy Mamabolo was elected Brits's first black mayor. ODT's Jacob Moatshe recalls that this was a hugely popular decision:

> Levy had a passion for development, human rights, worker rights. He was not corruptible and ran the Council without corruption. As a politician he was selfless. He was detained twice during the State of Emergency and he went on hunger strike even though he was a diabetic and

he developed abscesses and we feared he would collapse. He was a lovable person who worked well with white officials. There was a lot of delivery of services.[148]

One of Mamabolo's great contributions was, like Mandela's, the idea of reconciliation. Comments from the time reveal that white councillors and officials had confidence in him, which allayed white fears more generally in Brits. He also had a common touch, which allowed him to keep faith with his black constituency. He avoided the luxuries associated with later mayors, as Selepe recalls:

> He moved on his own feet. He caught a taxi home and walked to his house in Oukasie. Only on official trips did he use municipal transport. People were pleased as he identified himself as part of the working class.

Some prominent activists, however, decided not to enter the Council. Selepe recalls that some shop stewards were sceptical, especially as they wanted to influence decisions, but this was not easy because they were confronted at Council caucuses with a wide range of organisations. In Selepe's opinion:

> It was a mistake [not to be part of the Council], as a lot of younger, more inexperienced people came in, but on the other hand it meant we [NUMSA members] were never in a position to be tempted by greener pastures and to line our pockets. We tried to influence on the side-lines but we were generally not part of institutional arrangements.

Levy Mamabolo's Transitional Council did indeed deliver

services, but some of the problems that were later to haunt the Madibeng Council were already present in the TLC. South African local government income has traditionally been generated chiefly through rates, payment for services, taxes and small grants from national and provincial government for specific infrastructure. Commerce and industry contributed large amounts to this.[149] The white areas of Brits had benefitted greatly under apartheid because they were located near industrial areas and were wealthy enough to pay for services. They also benefitted from the enormous disparity in expenditure on the minority white areas in contrast to the majority black townships and villages which the NP serviced only minimally. After 1994, the ANC aimed to create unified cities with a centralised tax base which would service all citizens.

Black local authorities were bankrupt and attempted to squeeze black residents for income. In consequence, local councillors were viewed as sell-outs and bitterly disliked. In response, impoverished township residents across the country, unable to pay for services and without the benefits of local taxes, boycotted rental and service payments from the early 1980s onwards. The boycott in Oukasie, however, was only seriously observed in the late 1980s, despite YCW attempts to encourage one at an earlier date, because residents were focused on resisting removal.

Brits's tax base from TLC days onwards was not sufficient to provide new local infrastructure and ensure ongoing maintenance, especially as councils struggled to break the payment boycott culture. Municipalities were provided with some infrastructural grants from the national fiscus but maintenance work had to be paid for by local rates and taxes. Under the NP, provinces had subsidised rural development, but from 1995 onwards municipal income generated from industry had to subsidise the rural hinterland.[150]

After the 1995 municipal elections, the boundaries of the Brits Council expanded to include Brits town, Oukasie, Lethlabile, Mothutlung and surrounding villages. There was optimism and the Council led by Levy Mamabolo worked hard. In addition, the ANC's Reconstruction and Development Programme (RDP) put development at the centre of municipal objectives. The NP's Japie Steenkamp, who sat on the town's Transitional Council, acknowledged, "The council did good things. It got water to many villages and electricity... I worked with Levy [Mamabolo] on a good budget."[151] Unfortunately, the wise guidance of Mamabolo came to a sudden end when he died in March 1997 after just over three years on the Council. From this point Mamabolo's transparent manner of operating, which included open debate on local government issues and on how to allocate the budget, was progressively eroded. "Now there are budget meetings and no one is invited," commented Sello Selepe. Many of those interviewed for this book believed that there was a steady decline in the provision of services from this point onwards.

The YCW, NUMSA and many other community members believed that David Modimoeng was Mamabolo's natural successor considering his YCW, NUMSA and ANC organisational experience, and they confidently nominated him. By this time, however, the Council had become a political battleground for different ANC factions seeking to gain power and access to resources. NUMSA trade unionist Solly Phetoe recalls how politics coalesced around Modimoeng:

The early TLC was good and run by respected people. It did its best to bring services. We wanted David [Modimoeng] as mayor and there was support from some councillors and workers and even by opposition members but a faction in the ANC – anti-worker, ambitious for power – wanted him out. He was elected and became mayor for six months. The ANC faction took his position as mayor to court on the basis that the party had not nominated him on the consolidated list, and this was an IEC [Independent Electoral Commission] requirement – that you can show you were nominated by the ANC. It was an omission or deliberate. But either way, they got him out on a technicality.[152]

Sello Selepe, then local chairperson of the Congress of South African Trade Unions (COSATU), had been instrumental in getting Modimoeng released by NUMSA to stand for Council mayor. He appealed to Valli Moosa, Minister for Provincial and Constitutional Affairs, to intervene in these political manipulations. "But there was a cabal and we did not win, so David never played a pivotal role."

Council sidelines activists and the white right

A number of the old guard continued to try to assist and influence the Council's activities from the outside. Jacob Moatshe recalls that the ODT had drawn up development plans for the wider Bojanelo district but Mamabolo's successors were not interested. The Council rejected external assistance. This showed that it did not welcome the ODT's promotion of the Greater Brits Development Forum (GBDF) to plan economic development in the area.

Churches, industrialists, trade unionists and community consultants sat on the GBDF. Moatshe explained, "We developed a plan to 2030 and what resources were needed. But it was thwarted and died. There was a clash of visions even though industrialists put a lot into it."

Bert Badenhorst was convinced that if industry declined, Brits would die. He recalled that after 1994 he put much effort into the Brits Industrial Association (later the Madibeng Business Forum) which replaced the Sakekamer as the main industry forum. Development, he argued, was just as much about assisting business and industry as it was about developing residential areas. The Association included industry, trade unions and the National African Federated Chamber of Commerce and Industry (NAFCOC). It attempted to hold monthly meetings with the Council and be recognised as a formal support structure. But, as Badenhorst recalls, it failed.

> The Council is at the core of industry's problems. Council paid lip service to it [the Brits Industrial Association]. It went well with Levy [Mamabolo] but thereafter the mayor started being absent. Levy died and A.D. Ratlou, then [Raymond] Motsepe followed and it slid downwards. We created the North West Business Forum – I was vice president – to try and deal with industry's problems in the province. We tried to tell the [provincial] premier she must play a more definite role at local level.
>
> Electricity rates were raised very high, and Firestone and Autocast considered moving to the Eastern Cape. We are finished if we lose industrialists, as 70% of finance for the municipality comes from industry and business. The electricity infrastructure is over 40 years old. The

substations blew and we had no electricity for days in the early 2000s. We needed about R60 million to upgrade infrastructure. We approached the Development Bank to support a loan to upgrade and they said they could do it but wanted to administer the funds. The Council refused. I got so tired of trying. They knew everything.

The current mayor [2012] spent R500 000 on her inaugural party and R300 000 on Mandela Day and bought a new BMW. Local government is not healthy. It ignores inputs, refuses to cooperate, they don't react to emails or phone calls. If Rustenburg and Brits decline, the North West declines.[153]

Japie Steenkamp, still a National Party councillor, experienced similar frustration:

On the TLC we were about 25 councillors and eight to 10 were white, the rest black… The naming of streets in Lethlabile … the Ward Council allocates names and then brings them to the Council and they would argue for two days over names and everyone wanted a say. I thought, 'I'd rather go fishing, and I hate fishing' There was too much emotion and 'we'll do what we want'. A leader must do things that people don't like and not just be emotive.

Whites bypass the Council. They have water tanks, generators, four-by-fours that get over potholes, but small business will die without electricity. A huge number of people wanted to offer help but we were not accommodated. Many people are committed in industry. We don't want money. We just want to make a contribution, but eventually people started saying, 'Let's just stop paying…'

> *Jy moet lankmoedig wees* (you must be patient) to get anywhere. They [the Council] relaunched the Growth and Development Plan. Why? We did this four years ago [2008] and there has been not one report in four years. All reports start with, 'We aim to... We envisage... We plan to...' not with 'We did...'

The 1980s generation of black activists had moved through a process of developing their leadership and had gathered skills and confidence. When they led the removal struggle or planned development as part of the ODT, they were able to invite the participation of white managerial and technical outsiders and to use their skills for the benefit of Oukasie. The decline in participation of this generation left a gap. Black councillors were progressively younger, and they had not developed experience and confidence through participation in building organisation in the 1980s. Caroline Mashike, who had some ODT experience, recalls:

> I was one of the first democratically elected councillors. It was tough. I knew nothing. I was like a child. I learned about how to implement development and how to take care of money through the Municipal Finance Act.[154]

These councillors were learning the difficult task of governance on the job. TLC minutes reflect a focus on training councillors in workshops, including on human rights in local government, national water regulations, housing, planning and development and town planning. This training was often provided by the District Council Eastern Region, particularly in the early days.[155]

Many councillors viewed offers of outside help,

particularly from whites, as a threat and an intrusion. Badenhorst, Steenkamp and others like them were reaping what they had sown over the long years of apartheid. People were suspicious of their motives. For white representatives, a discussion on renaming streets seemed irrelevant, while for these new black councillors the power to rename streets after heroes of the struggle held huge symbolic significance.[156]

Troubled finances and delivery

The TLC began the process of delivering services to neglected townships and to some rural communities. Servicing rural areas continued and expanded under the Madibeng Council established in 2000. By 2005 Brits's rural hinterland was electrified (except for two villages) and 90% of households had running water in their yards. The TLC had to persuade rural communities to start paying for services, but poor villagers in places like Maboloka and Jericho, receiving services for the first time, were reluctant to pay the R75 per month levy.[157] Meanwhile, in urban townships the service boycott persisted. The Council began taking legal steps against consumers in arrears, and by 1998 it started to suspend water supply, charging a R945 reconnection fee.* Council minutes record that they had some success in breaking the non-payment culture.[158]

The Brits Council supported the national Masakhane project launched by President Mandela in 1995.[159] The project aimed to address socio-economic challenges, promote full citizenship through participation and develop

---

* National government provided 25 litres of free water per person per day; thereafter non-payment resulted in drip water only.

new ways of thinking and acting.[160] For many councils, however, the hope that the promise of inclusive citizenship would persuade people to pay for services was written off as a failure by 1999, including by the Brits Council.[161] Non-payment by some meant that the Council had to increase tariffs excessively on an annual basis to continue providing sufficient services, but increases simply led to further non-payment.[162]

By 1999 the Brits TLC noted a serious financial cash-flow crisis to the tune of R40 526 227, which meant it was unable to pay R11 815 830 owed to contractors. Before the 1994 elections, the Council held millions of rand in investments (particularly in Sanlam and Old Mutual), but a decision to trade such equity to settle debts soon eroded the Council's financial security.[163] By the 2000 municipal elections, all investments had been recalled and the Council moved relentlessly towards bankruptcy.[164]

Sello Selepe believed that further development in Oukasie was deliberately neglected by the Council. He argued that interracial political integration on the TLC occurred but that the administration was still dominated by whites. In consequence, most development went to Lethlabile and surrounds. "In Oukasie, up until today the infrastructure was provided by the TPA. Only a few houses have been built since then, and that falls under the province anyway. This was punishment for Oukasie's refusal to move." Selepe's comment only holds partial truth. TLC minutes in the early days reflect a concern with continuing Oukasie's development initiated by the ODT. The Council, for instance, acted as a conduit for the Department of Land Affairs to donate land to the north of Oukasie for development, and it facilitated the transfer of land from the old South African Development Trust to the TLC for use in Oukasie. It also budgeted R1 591 000 for this expansion and development, and set aside R50 000 to provide floodlights for Oukasie's communal sports fields and R200 000 for the erection of shelters at the Oukasie taxi rank.[165] In its January 1996 budget it included an amount over the following 10 years to ensure a bulk electricity supply to Oukasie.[166] It is clear, however, that if the ODT had not made a massive contribution to Oukasie prior to 1994, it would still lack the most basic amenities.

It is noticeable that much of the infrastructural upgrading during the Brits Transitional Council era occurred in the 1996–1997 period – that is, in Levy Mamabolo's time. However, this massive early expenditure may be linked to the Council's rapid move into bankruptcy by the late 1990s.

Balancing delivery to rural and urban areas

As the Council matured, all the towns it covered revealed maintenance oversights accompanied by rising service costs. The reasons were complex and included bad planning, lack of skills and inadequate income streams. In part, Bert Badenhorst's fears were realised when some industry moved to Ga-Rankuwa, Rosslyn and Johannesburg, where power and transport costs were cheaper. These companies included Van Leer, Autocast and African Telephone Cables, which left 5 000 people without jobs (despite NUMSA's spirited engagement with the Council and government on job losses). The days of super-subsidisation for Bantustan border industries were over.

The issue of water purification illustrates the seriousness of this decline. The TLC realised that raw sewage was entering local rivers and that the existing water purification works were insufficient to service a growing population. An engineer's report addressed the problem, but instead of tackling the sewage leaks the Council decided to employ people to make sure that the taste and odour of the water were all right.[167] But as Japie Steenkamp explained, the problem lay elsewhere:

> There are two pumps – one in use and one in case of breakdown. The Council used the second one and sent the other for repairs… Then the Council said it did not have money to get it back from the engineers.

He contended that the pressure to support rural development meant the Council lost sight of critical infrastructure repairs, which were capital intensive. Advanced planning became impossible.

A Madibeng Council employee believed that infrastructural maintenance neglect was in part due to councillors' short-term attitudes. They saw that the infrastructure was working and assumed it would operate indefinitely. Typically, the maintenance budget line was the easiest to cut, especially as politicians promised to supply expanded infrastructure to their constituencies. The ODT culture of informing and consultation through community general meetings, where finances and their deployment were discussed, was not emulated by the Council. Soon "maintenance" became "crisis management". If a pipe burst over a weekend, an external service provider was called at double the rates. Over time the Council's maintenance department was underused and became weaker.

By 2009 Lethlabile residents were experiencing frequent

water shortages, which the TLC had predicted and which the Madibeng Council seemed unable to resolve.* Since the early 1990s there had been a large population increase in the area. This was due to mass evictions of farm workers in the wake of the Labour Relations Act in 1995 and the introduction of a Sectoral Determination for Farm Workers stipulating minimum wages in 2002. Moreover, economic migrants from elsewhere in Africa began moving into the area. Mamabolo noted in his ODT report that in 1995 Oukasie's population stood at 12 000 while two years later it had almost doubled to 22 000.[168] Brits's overstretched purification plant had to provide for this increased population and also deliver water to a massive new housing development immediately to the north-west of Lethlabile. Because of this, Lethlabile's reservoir, which was supplied by the main Brits reservoir, frequently ran dry. The pressure on the infrastructure was simply too great. Another factor was that some politicians – wanting to be elected – made the popular promise to provide, for instance, street lighting in the face of the more urgent need to expand water purification works.

Trade unionist Peter Magagula claims that the "delivery of services was good in the 1990s" despite Brits's increase in population during the time of the TLC.[169] The Council's target population, however, became even greater after the 2000 elections and the formation of the new municipality.

During the time of the TLC, a Demarcation Board met regularly to create "wall to wall" councils across the country in time for municipal elections. The new demarcations brought together huge rural areas and towns

---

* Ironically, Madibeng means "place of water" in Setswana, and Brits's motto in apartheid times had been *Lewe vanuit water* – Life from water.

not previously covered by the Council. This spelled disaster for the Council, which was already stretched financially. The new Brits Council, now the Madibeng Council (which also covered Oukasie), stretched over an area of 3 814 square kilometres; it had 36 wards, of which 10 fell within urban areas and 21 in rural areas and villages.[170]

Before 1994 Brits and Hartbeespoort were separate councils. The new demarcation now incorporated Hartbeespoort as another tax base for the post-2000 council of Madibeng. Hartbeespoort residents, sensing declining services, resisted and took the issue to court but did not win.[171]

Council corruption: Politics and union response

Many in Lethlabile believed that corruption was at the root of the water problems.[172] Lethlabile resident and former member of the Brits Action Committee (BAC) Caleb Dube explained that to alleviate the water scarcity, tankers entered the community. People pushed wheelbarrows carrying water containers to a collection point and sometimes had to pay for water. The Council contracted out the delivery of water so, Dube believed, some people had a vested interest in not solving water shortages.[173] Corruption was the most common way that people explained the lack of services, but many factors were at play.

Yet the corruption factor in the post-Mamabolo Council was clearly an added obstruction to the delivery of services. There is evidence in later TLC meeting minutes that the Council was aware of growing corruption among councillors and took some steps to prevent it. In the early days, free use of photocopy facilities, especially for ANC party functionaries, was forbidden.[174] Later, the use of Council cars for councillors doing private business was forbidden, and councillors were disciplined and charged if they broke these rules.[175] In 1998 the town secretary was tasked with providing a code of conduct for councillors who had "pecuniary interests in contracts with the Council". The abuse of tenders was clearly emerging as an issue.[176] At the time, it was councillors who decided on the allocation of tenders – a function that was later removed to a separate committee. TLC minutes record that in April 1999 Councillor Masela had not declared his interest in Bathopele Construction [sic] which tendered for Council work and was awarded a contract of R245 000. The Council cancelled the tender and the process recommenced.[177] In June of the same year, two councillors – S. Chauke and J.T.P. de Jager – also broke the code and were disciplined.[178]

On the Madibeng Council, such abuse became more serious with the introduction of municipal managers. The ANC in government championed the New Public Management (NPM) model which emphasised an entrepreneurial spirit to transform the public service. The NPA advocated a corporate model, with managers in control instead of accountable leadership working according to policies and rules. These managers were given considerable powers, including handling contracts, cash, budgets and staff. Government generally, and in Madibeng specifically, struggled to find suitable candidates with the range of skills required, and officials were thus often set up for failure.[179] In this disempowered environment some individuals engaged in corrupt activities to acquire individual wealth.

A Madibeng official spoke of how the Council would allocate money for development, and soon after a further request for money would be submitted as "only a third of the project was completed and money had been syphoned off. This would not appear in Council minutes because procedure required that it be put on the agenda, which seldom occurred, or Council officials reported it to the police and the dossier was either negligently or deliberately lost."[180]

Local politics also became entangled with provincial political manoeuvring and corruption. Housing, for example, was a provincial dispensation so Members of the [provincial] Executive Council (MECs) used the delivery of housing to gather mass support. Sello Selepe believed the faction-ridden ANC politics of the North West province affected municipal delivery:

> In the district Bojanelo it depended which faction you were in, so one mayor sabotaged another and simply didn't attend meetings when they wanted to sabotage. It was personalised, and destabilised service delivery not driven by ideology but to amass personal wealth. It's driven by greed and graft.

A great deal of information about corruption began to emerge from the South African Municipal Workers' Union (SAMWU) from 2005 onwards. Their members worked in the Council and directly encountered fraud. Oukasie's Jacob Modimoeng, a former member of the YCW and a brother to David Modimoeng, was the provincial secretary of SAMWU North West. He explained that shop stewards began to receive requests from members to deal with corruption on the Madibeng Council. However, when shop stewards raised problems with managers, they were often dismissed. Senior SAMWU employees were especially affected, as they worked in the finance department and had direct access to financial records where they encountered tender and other fraud. [181]

Corruption also showed itself in smaller ways. For instance, a Council manager owned a company, and when his trucks needed repair he would get the Council's maintenance department to do repairs for nothing. Service delivery was often outsourced to friends or family members of councillors, even when the municipality had the capacity to deliver the service itself. Corruption combined with inefficiency had a bad effect on the town's routine maintenance. Over a three-month period in 2010, for instance, workers in the Roads and Technical Services Division were unable to work because all tractors and equipment were not functioning or had missing parts.

Workers clocked in every day at the Madibeng Council and remained idle as garbage piled up around the town. In this way, corrupt managers involved in outsourcing services directly threatened their jobs. Whistle-blowing also frequently ended in dismissal. Attacks on union functionaries were directly political because SAMWU members were employed by the ANC in government, so when workers exposed ANC officials it involved ANC politics. The ANC ensured loyalty by directly appointing politicians, such as mayors, after its victories in the 2000, 2006 and 2011 municipal elections. In the ANC's eyes, SAMWU members were disloyal because they questioned corruption and the maladministration of the people it had deployed. Those loyal to SAMWU were dismissed, while those who pledged loyalty to the ANC kept their jobs.

Jacob Modimoeng commented, "Attacks on SAMWU are sometimes framed as a political issue but, in fact, it's to cover up corruption."

SAMWU informed local ANC branches about the corruption in the Council, but they showed no interest in pursuing it. It also met with provincial premiers but, again, no action was taken. SAMWU, the South African Communist Party (SACP), the South African National Civic Organisation (SANCO) and COSATU delivered a report to Sicelo Shiceka, the Minister of Cooperative Governance and Traditional Affairs, in 2009 on the corruption plaguing North West municipalities including Madibeng. Shiceka established an investigative task team but, until his death in 2012, refused to release the report. In Madibeng only one corrupt municipal manager was dismissed, according to Modimoeng.

> He is now treasurer of the ANC in the province. He is a corrupt man who swindled the Council out of thousands...
> There is a blurring of the ANC and the state. We are a poor province and only COSATU is ringing the bell.

In 2009 an acting chief finance officer, Nana Masithela, was appointed to the Madibeng municipality. Unionists believed he was incompetent and corrupt, and the Council ground to a halt. In February 2010, SAMWU members went on strike for three weeks and demanded Masithela's removal. They also demanded that the mayor stop the outsourcing of services which municipal workers could render.

Meanwhile, people in communities around Brits – in particular Oukasie, Mothutlung and Lethlabile – protested about deteriorating services. In 2010 a group of six residents joined the striking SAMWU workers and organised the largest-ever protest march of 15 000 people through Brits. They demanded better roads, clean and accessible water and other services, and also that mayor Sophie Molokoane-Machika, resign. It was a significant action because such solidarity between unions and the community had not occurred since the early 1990s. Their demands were not met, however, and services continued to deteriorate.[182]

Post-apartheid: Protest continues in Oukasie

In spite of the increasing distance between communities and the trade unions that operated in Brits after 1994, community protest was still alive. In Lethlabile, from 2009 onwards, different groups embarked on demonstrations against water shortages. In 2010 youth in Oukasie staged a similar protest to demand better service delivery; in a confrontation with police 148 were arrested for public violence.[183]

In October 2011 taxi operators from Brits, Oukasie, Lethlabile and Maboloka demonstrated by driving slowly to the traffic department in Brits to demand permanent passenger licences in place of the temporary licences which they had to pay for and renew on a monthly basis.[184] In September 2011 Oukasie government administration offices near the township were stoned and damaged during a demonstration to protest crumbling township infrastructure and rising crime.[185]

A feature of these protests was that the instigators were often former ANC councillors hoping to be reappointed, on whom disgruntled residents piggybacked. In Lethlabile a group calling itself Concerned Citizens was led by former ANC councillors who, together with militant youths in the area, were responsible for organising demonstrations.[186] A July 2011 study by the Centre for the Study of Violence and Reconciliation (CSVR) investigated violence and protest in a number of communities. Their report concluded, "There were variations in the composition of protest organisers across the case studies, but a similarity in the leading role played by ANC figures in all of them."[187]

By 2010 services had deteriorated so badly in townships around Brits that protest was becoming a feature of township life. In the first decade of 2000, the Madibeng Council had declined so much in its ability to deliver services that a 2010 research report by Ratings Afrika concluded that Madibeng was the lowest-scoring municipality in the country.[188] As its ratings allowed banks to assess the merit of lending to municipalities to supplement their budgets, this was disastrous for the Council. By 2009 Madibeng was so badly mismanaged by dishonest and incompetent political appointees that the province placed it under administration until May 2011. Protests continued, as the new administrator proved to be incompetent.[189]

Communities in Oukasie, Lethlabile and other areas of the Madibeng municipality are mobilised. Yet their activism does not compare with the robust solidarity and organisational engagement of the early 1980s and 1990s led by the YCW, trade unions, the ODT and civic organisations. A marked difference is the lack of unity within and between communities. According to former NUMSA unionist Sello Ramakobye, "Different groups organise different things. Organisation is splintered. There is no unity so meetings are not productive. Former councillors want to sabotage the current Council." Peter Magagula, who lives in Lethlabile, noted the lack of contact between Oukasie and Lethlabile, partly because of their histories but also because unity of purpose and the hard work entailed to forge this does not lie at the heart of current action. Hlokoza Motau is disturbed that local ANC organisation does not build leadership in the way unions and the YCW did in the past, and that people are afraid to take organising initiatives.

> The ANC deals with procedure, not substantive issues, and it doesn't capacitate people as in the 1980s ... there is no sense of community. Oukasie was the home of all meetings. Now people fear that if they organise there will be a backlash. They fear violence from ANC comrades.[190]

People have lost confidence in their ability to achieve change through organisation and to be heard by local leadership. Leadership is drowning in a culture of self-interest and this "spirit of enriching yourself is very difficult for us, and people with bad backgrounds get into leadership," commented Magagula. He believes people's lack of empowerment leads them into blindly supporting people. "We like to worship people, who later disappoint," he said. Ramakobye supports this view of local leadership: "Incompetent people were put in, and we put anyone in as we were caught up in the euphoria, and we did not have skills but wanted to keep positions."

For the old activists, the current populist organisations which focus on confronting authorities are as problematic now as they were in the 1980s. There is no more strategic discussion around alliances to work with to further goals because such autonomy is not encouraged by the ANC.

Sello Selepe remarked:

> Protest shows a lack of leadership. It is driven by young people who use violence, so it is easy for the authorities to squash it. Then another group mobilises. Unions don't work with the community except for SAMWU where delivery must happen. We work with anyone as in the Egoli 2000 campaign against privatisation, but the ANC said we work with counter-revolutionaries...

Caleb Dube, who sat on the ward council committee in Lethlabile, is concerned that, despite the growing population in townships, the Madibeng Council appears to have no coherent plan:

> The IDP [Integrated Development Plan] is not working properly. I give monthly reports to ward councillors who take the report to the municipality but it makes no difference ... but even if the ward's voice is not loud, the little government does is better than nothing... But there are a lot of DA [Democratic Alliance] supporters in the township.

The ANC lost the new ward 21, which included part of Oukasie's Vuka Section, all of Elandsrand and Damonsville, to the Democratic Alliance in the 2014 elections.

Dube has pinpointed that effective delivery requires ANC leadership to carefully listen to its cadres on the ground. Nobel laureate Amartya Sen has noted that there are problems in achieving justice entirely in institutional terms because people come to consider institutions as inviolable quite aside from what they actually deliver:

But what if … 'just institutions' generate terrible results for the people in that society?… The … issue is the basic unreliability of not being constantly sensitive to what is happening in the world… To ask how things are going and whether they can be improved is a constant and inescapable part of the pursuit of justice.[191]

In small ways the legacy of those early, vibrant activists lives on. Some of them are still making their presence felt in the arena of social justice and provision to the poor, both inside and outside of Brits. They are still asking "how things are going and whether they can be improved" as they offer critiques supported by organisational experience. Yet, as Peter Magagula poignantly expressed it, it is not always easy to make a contribution:

> We need to help councillors, as we are older and more experienced, but there is a huge gap with older people. They [young councillors] don't know us. We have not given continuity in our history. They look at us as opportunists. There are very young people in Council … who want to see results now … money is the only interest… We feel helpless. And unfortunately, lots of guys are cynical and disillusioned.

Celebrating the YCW

On 26 November 1995 the South African YCW welcomed 130 delegates of the International YCW to the opening ceremony of its IX World Council. It was held in Oukasie, where the movement had played such an unforgettable role. Newly elected President Nelson Mandela was invited to take part in the ceremony as nearly every resident gathered on the township soccer field. In a moving tribute to the YCW Mandela said:

> One of the YCW's most important characteristics is that it situated itself in the social realities of people ... and places strong emphasis on effective organisation. Our decades of struggle, outside and inside prison, taught us that the most important tool of resistance is proper organisation... YCW's emphasis on active participation of its members in developing plans to change their lives has proved to have great potential for capacity-building among our youth.[192]

Nelson Mandela dances to music of Woza Africa on an Oukasie soccer field at the Young Christian Workers IX World Council in 1995. (Photo: Getty Images)

The Brits Oukasie story is an inspiring tale of how deeply disempowered people took command of their lives. The emergence of a small organisation in the early 1980s – the YCW and the trade unions it engaged with, in particular the metal unions – resulted in the development of a democratic leadership and a critical consciousness which strengthened people's power to change their destiny. This they did through committed action guided by strategic thinking, as reflected in their motto: See, Judge and Act.

Oukasie's anti-removal struggle placed the community at the centre of inspiration and innovation as people fought the monster of latter-day apartheid and grasped the opportunity to use whatever resources were available. One of the strengths of its leadership was to employ service organisations and non-governmental organisations who supported their struggles. This enabled them to go beyond resistance and to engage in a major reconstruction project.

Little did these determined people know that their powerful struggle to remain in Oukasie, where they belonged, would lead them to providing the first effective black "municipal" services through the ODT. Sadly, it has been the new democratic South Africa that has ended all this. The new Madibeng municipality under which Oukasie falls has become divorced from the guidance of its communities in the way that the YCW, the BAC, the OCA and the ODT so clearly understood. Over time, a self-interested Council that was unable to share with its communities the difficult constraints it works under has been incapable of delivering a just and democratic dispensation to its constituency.

SIX
Afterword

THIS STORY OF THE STRUGGLE of Oukasie's residents to claim their living space has placed organisation at its centre. The Young Christian Workers (YCW), which targeted young people and initiated this battle, has existed on the margins of labour and struggle histories. This book places the YCW, as well as the trade unions and other organisations in which they participated, at the centre of the narrative, and reveals a political tradition that emerged in the struggle against apartheid which posed an alternative to organisations like the South African Communist Party (SACP) and the United Democratic Front (UDF).

Rooted in a socialist interpretation of Christianity, these young workers rejected the high-profile protest action and populist rhetoric of youth organisations like the Congress of South African Students (COSAS) and followed an independent path. They were guided by the method of "See, Judge and Act", which entailed the development of an informed, reflective and strategic programme of participatory action to bring change. This approach developed a mature and accountable leadership. The YCW's approach meshed with the emerging independent trade union movement, creating a leadership which guided Oukasie's resistance to removal in the 1980s and engaged in bottom-up infrastructural development in the early 1990s.

The meaning of Oukasie's struggle

Interviews took place and other information was gathered for this book during 2011 and 2012. Much of the book tells of the impressive struggles and achievements of a creative, politicised and mobilised community in the 1980s and 1990s. Chapter 5, however, talks about the descent of the Madibeng Council, under which Oukasie falls, into corruption and decay. This in turn has generated fragmented protest by Oukasie residents and neighbouring communities.

While Oukasie still boasts some solid infrastructure, its increased population has meant a growth in the number of zinc shacks in the recently formed Zone 3 informal settlement. Post-apartheid, people from neighbouring rural and semi-rural areas such as Maboloka, Jericho, Bapong, Soshanguve and Ga-Rankuwa, as well as foreign nationals from other African countries, have moved into Oukasie. They are attracted by its infrastructure and its nearness to the Brits city centre. The Madibeng Council has only minimally serviced this growing section of the township.

The malfunctioning Council was put under provincial administration in 2009, but this was lifted after the May 2011 municipal elections. However, by 2014 Madibeng was again under administration, accompanied by an escalation in service-delivery protests.

The current Madibeng mayor, Jostine Mothibe, was appointed after the lifting of the provincial administration. However, little servicing has occurred and the Council's financial woes have continued. In December 2017 it owed R60 million to bulk water suppliers and R40 million to Eskom for electricity. Mothibe has been accused of corruption and high living, including owning a guesthouse in Brits that is a popular venue for municipal activities and renting a car for municipal business at the cost of R100 000 per month, despite the Council buying her a BMW in 2014.[193] Such leadership has continued to promote an atmosphere of corrupt practices that have seeped into the fabric of the council.

The South African Municipal Workers' Union (SAMWU) has persisted in its attempts to expose corruption, but its relationship with ANC councillors has continued to deteriorate. A recent refusal by the Council to produce what appeared to be a fraudulent municipal vehicle leasing contract led to the municipal manager assaulting a SAMWU official who was requesting a copy of the contract.[194]

In May 2017 hundreds of Oukasie residents marched to the Madibeng municipal offices to hand over a memorandum demanding promised service delivery. The memorandum stated that Oukasie was suffering under crime, unemployment, poverty, bad roads and pit latrines. Residents reminded the Council that it had promised to remove building rubble concealing criminals, to deliver 1 500 houses, to demarcate stands and to provide more high-mast lights to help fight crime.[195] There was little response from the municipality.

The provincial administration's failure to improve Madibeng's performance was due in part to the rotten state of the provincial authority itself. Guided by premier Supra Mahumapelo, himself tarnished by corruption allegations, the North West province erupted in violent protest in April 2018, forcing him to resign. In an unprecedented move, President Cyril Ramaphosa placed the entire North West province under the control of the national government, including many local and district municipalities.[196]

Such leadership contrasts markedly with the Oukasie leadership of the past, which was embedded in the trade unions and the community. The leaders in those days took their mandate from, and reported back to, a community that guided their actions. It existed in the context of solidarity and mutual benefit, where leadership did its best to deliver to its constituency. Individual success, promotion and enrichment were not its goal.

Post-apartheid leadership in the Council, however, emerged from a different ethos. A corporate model of public administration, governed by powerful managers, takes precedence over accountable leadership. Former Oukasie leaders represented the community's demands, shared strategic thinking and planning and guided its actions. They were able to recognise where they lacked skills and to draw on supportive outsiders to guide technical decisions and practices. However, these outside practitioners were subject to the control of the community. This two-way accountability yielded startlingly positive results in both the removal struggle and in the later development of Oukasie.

Many of the officials in the post-apartheid Brits and Madibeng transitional councils were not embedded in the community in the same way. They only heard the voices of the communities they served when protest erupted – a situation that did not lend itself to representation and consultation. A younger generation of officials had emerged in an environment where the necessity to build organisation and win victories through consultation, solidarity and compromise had not been learned in the cauldron of struggle. Youth in Oukasie now reproduce the anti-apartheid popular protest tool of ungovernability – the model which the YCW and the Federation of South African Trade Unions had rejected.

After acknowledging the grievances of protesters, Madibeng councillors return to the comfort of their council chambers. For the former Oukasie leadership, follow-up to protest had been as important as the protest action itself in order to maintain pressure on government and to sustain a spirit of unity and resistance. Their persistence engaged the state for prolonged periods, allowing for a shift to a new political moment in which Oukasie was saved from being destroyed by removals. This permitted genuine development to unfold.

The difference in the outcomes achieved by Oukasie activists during and after apartheid suggests the need for the militants of today to reflect on the organisational principles and leadership approaches that underpinned Oukasie's engagement with the state, fortified by a strong community mandate.

Where have they gone?

What happened to the once powerful Oukasie leaders from the YCW and the National Union of Metalworkers of South Africa (NUMSA)?

Company relocations and massive job losses in the manufacturing sector have reduced NUMSA's power in the area. SAMWU, whose members in the Madibeng municipality directly observe corrupt activities, has taken over from NUMSA. As the public sector and mining grew in Brits, the ranks of SAMWU and the National Union of Mineworkers (NUM) swelled and became more powerful in local union structures. Inevitably, NUMSA's strong leadership moved beyond the confines of small-town Brits. Some activists have remained in NUMSA, or in the trade union movement, but they are no longer a commanding local team available to mentor young new Oukasie leadership. Its experienced leaders have moved into the national structures of NUMSA as well as the Congress of South African Trade Unions (COSATU) and the South African Federation of Trade Unions (SAFTU), into company human resources departments, into ANC and government structures and into business. And with these shifts has come a dilution of the socialist perspective of the unions and the YCW.

Peter Dantjies, a YCW member and an early B&S organiser, was elected Assistant General Secretary of NUMSA, later became its Northern Transvaal regional secretary and moved into business after 1994. Hlokoza Motau became NUMSA's international officer in the head office in Johannesburg, while Sello Ramakobye, who had been transferred to Firestone's Port Elizabeth branch to escape threats on his life, returned to and later retired in Oukasie. NUMSA's July Khoza now works for the municipality, and Sello Selepe shifted to SAMWU, becoming its North West provincial chairperson.

Some YCW leadership who had not entered the unions

also moved into prominent positions. Tshidi Mangoathe became a councillor and then mayor, although her stay in office was short.[197] Jacob Moatshe remained with the ODT (later the Platinum Development Trust) and then assisted in establishing the Madibeng Centre for Research in partnership with the University of Pretoria. The Centre conducts clinical trials for HIV, tuberculosis and other diseases to service local communities, mines and farm areas.

Tshidi Mangoathe, an early YCW activist and trade unionist, became mayor in 2012 but could not withstand the corrupt municipal environment. (Photo: K Forrest)

Despite some former YCW and union activists remaining in the trade unions, their dynamic link with community issues has disappeared. Taffy Adler recalls that NUMSA's informal link with the ODT had already faded in the early 1990s once "the glue – the threat of removal" had disappeared and Sello Ramakobye, who sat on the ODT Board, had moved away.[198] Also, as Hlokoza Motau lamented, "We had energy because we were young – meeting seven days a week."[199] Retirement, old age and death had taken its toll.

David Modimoeng returned to NUMSA as an organiser until his death in 2008. Jean-Marie Dumortier gave this tribute at Modimoeng's funeral: "Yes, I am sad to let you go today. You fought for Truth, Justice, Freedom and Solidarity. Long ago, in the Bible, people who were fighting for these very things were called 'Prophets'."[200] Levy Mamabolo also passed away in 1997, having never fully recovered from the neglected treatment of his diabetes while in detention. Mamabolo and Modimoeng's departure symbolised the declining influence of the older group of activists on the Council, individuals who were deeply and selflessly committed to justice.

In a political corruption scandal, the former chairperson of the Oukasie Civic Association and trustee of the Oukasie Development Trust, Phineas Ngale, took his life in July 2012. Moshe Mahlaela, treasurer of the Brits Action Committee and former shop steward for the National Automobile and Allied Workers' Union (NAAWU), has also passed away; he had applied for permission to build in Oukasie and thus triggered the successful legal action to force the Transvaal administration to allocate a site. B&S strike committee, Oukasie Women's Movement and Joint Parents Committee members Wanda Makgale and David Madumo are now retired in Oukasie, while Ellen Khoza is long deceased. ODT trustee Caroline Mashike has also retired and now lives in Mamelodi. Meanwhile Nankie Matlhare and Caleb Dube were both active in the

Oukasie taxi industry, and Dube is now operating a school bus service. Dumortier has left Oukasie and returned to France, and with this came the demise of the YCW and its meticulous and consultative leadership training. The YCW, with its worker-inflected focus, no longer operates in South Africa.

ANC politics had also affected the independence of some NUMSA leaders. As Jacob Modimoeng explained, "you cannot be loyal to both the union and the ANC because at times your members will demand that you critique, take action or reveal information that is not palatable to the ruling party." Sello Ramakobye believes that the ANC is intolerant of autonomous thinking, especially because of the corruption with which some ANC people have engaged. This made it difficult to discuss what was happening on the ground in ANC and union branch meetings. If you did, there were consequences, noted Solly Phetoe, a younger YCW member, NUMSA organiser and COSATU North West regional secretary:

> They, including NUMSA people, will campaign against you. NUMSA was diluted by ANC politics. The political situation in the North West has changed. We are under attack, especially affiliates of COSATU who were proactive in ANC branches and continued to advocate the NDR [National Democratic Revolution]. They were kicked out. They see me as the enemy, as I criticise them.[201]

Brits businessman Bert Badenhorst recalled a unionist complaining to him that "the ANC ignores us if we want to engage in development through local government."[202] Fear of assassination was also present, as people heard how Moss Phakoe – an Oukasie resident, NUMSA ATC shop steward, chair of the COSATU local and Rustenburg councillor – had been murdered. In 2009 Phakoe presented a report to the Council and to Sicelo Shiceka, Minister of Cooperative Governance at the time, containing allegations of tender corruption. Two days later Phakoe was shot dead outside his house in Rustenburg.* This contrasted markedly with the 1980s and early 1990s when justice and autonomous action drove NUMSA and the YCW, allowing them to act rapidly in the interest of their members without fear of factional violence.

However, despite the fragmentation of Oukasie's leadership in recent years, their footprints in Oukasie remain, even if hidden from a new generation of residents. Houses with flush toilets, water and title deeds, some tarred roads, the community hall, the library filled with brightly coloured books and tables and chairs for people to relax or work at, the clinic, the shaded taxi rank, electricity and some high-mast lighting are a living testimony to the

---

* At Phakoe's funeral Solly Phetoe, who worked with him in NUMSA, addressed 30 000 people in the Rustenburg Olympia Park stadium and swore to get justice. Suspicion fell on ANC mayor Matthew Wolmarans, who was implicated in the report. COSATU demonstrations in 2009 and 2010 demanded an enquiry. Wolmarans and his bodyguard were arrested in 2012; Wolmarans was sentenced to 20 years in prison and his bodyguard to life. Shortly before these convictions, Phineas Ngale, former ODT trustee and office manager to Wolmarans, shot himself and left a note saying, 'Tell M.J. Wolmarans I don't doubt his innocence.' Wolmarans was released a year later and has replaced disgraced Eskom CEO and former Member of Parliament Brian Molefe as an MP. The reason for Ngale's suicide is not clear. He had been questioned by the police about Phakoe's murder, and Wolmarans had been arrested in Ngale's car, which he had used to avoid arrest. COSATU continued to demand the release of the report that Phakoe gave to Shiceka and others but the ANC denied all knowledge of it. (Sources: Solly Phetoe, interview, 15 May 2012; *Mail & Guardian*, 27 July 2012; https://www.news24.com/SouthAfrica/News/controversial-anc-leader-goes-to-parliament-20170819.)

courageous, hard and imaginative work that these leaders of the past invested in the community to which they were bonded. Indeed, the very existence of Oukasie at all is in large part due to the actions of a leadership and community of people who refused to be moved.

Notes

Chapter 1

1. Brits Town Council, *Gedenk Album Brits 1924–1974*, 1974.
2. Bert Badenhorst, interview, 22 November 2011. All Badenhorst quotes in this chapter are from this interview.
3. Bosses move from homelands to escape from trade unions, *Fosatu Worker News*, Oct/Nov 1984.
4. Brits Town Council, *Gedenk Album*, p. 49.
5. Karl Catteeuw and Jos Dumortier (editors), *The Long Struggle Record of the YCWs in Africa: 75th Anniversary of the Young Christian Workers*, Brussels: International Cardijn Foundation, 2000.
6. Donovan Lowry, *20 Years in the Labour Movement*, Johannesburg: Wadmore, 1999, p. 25.
7. Lowry, *20 Years in the Labour Movement*, p. 46.
8. International Young Christian Workers (IYCW), *Declaration of Principles, 1975*, available at: sources.cardijncommunityaustralia.org/the (accessed 12 March 2012).
9. Catteeuw and Dumortier, *The Long Struggle*, p. 24.
10. Lowry, *20 Years in the Labour Movement*, p. 22.
11. Moses Cloete, interview, 25 October 2011. All Cloete quotes in this chapter are from this interview.
12. Email from Jacob Moatshe to Moses Cloete, 21 September 2009.
13. Hlokoza Motau, interview, 7 November 2011. All Motau quotes in this chapter are from this interview.
14. Jacob Moatshe, interview, 5 November 2011. All Moatshe quotes in this chapter are from this interview.
15. *Young Worker*, No. 16, 1989.
16. We want Genuine Representation, Young Christian Workers Campaign, 1980.

17. Peter Dantjies, interview, June 1997. All Dantjies quotes in this chapter are from this interview.
18. Jeremy Keenan, The B&S closure: Rationalisation or reprisal? *South African Labour Bulletin*, 10(1), 1984, p. 77.
19. Georgina Jaffee, Living with unemployment: Strategies for survival, *Work in Progress*, 34 (Oct), 1984, p. 16.
20. Keenan, The B&S closure.
21. Quoted in Kally Forrest, *Metal That Will Not Bend: National Union of Metal Workers of South Africa 1980–1995*, Johannesburg: Wits University Press, 2011, p. 111.
22. They're back, *Fosatu Worker News*, No. 25, October 1983; Keenan, The B&S closure.
23. Keenan, The B&S closure, pp. 77–98.
24. Keenan, The B&S closure, pp. 77–98.
25. Jean-Marie Dumortier, *Pour ne pas vous oublier: Prêtre en Afrique du sud*, Editions ouvrières (French Edition), 1991, p. 127.
26. Taffy Adler, interview, 7 December 2011. All Adler quotes in this chapter are from this interview.
27. We will not give in, *Fosatu Worker News*, May 1983.
28. Keenan, The B&S closure.
29. Dumortier, *Pour ne pas vous oublier*, p. 129.
30. Jaffee, Living with unemployment.
31. *The Struggle of the Workers at B&S Furniture Company*, video by Georgina Jaffee, directed by Edward Wes, 1993.
32. Dumortier, *Pour ne pas vous oublier*, p. 128.
33. Kally Forrest, Levy Mamabolo, the people's mayor, *South African Labour Bulletin*, 20(1), 1996.
34. Dumortier, Obituary for David Modimoeng, Cardijn Movement Newsfeed, 21 February 2009, available at http:cardijn.info/ccnew/cardjinmovement-news.
35. saycwstruggle.blogspot.com, 3 October 2012.

Chapter 2

36. Japie Steenkamp, interview, 15 February 2012. All Steenkamp quotes in this chapter are from this interview.
37. Leslie J. Banks, *Home Spaces, Street Styles: Contesting Power and Identity in a South African City*, London and Johannesburg: Pluto Press and Wits University, 2011.
38. Black Sash, *The Myth of Voluntary Removals*, Johannesburg: Black Sash, undated (1985?).
39. Laurine Platzky, Reprieves and repression: Relocation in South Africa, *South African Review 3*, Johannesburg: Ravan Press, 1986.
40. Deborah Newton, Forced removals in South Africa, *South African Review 5*, Johannesburg: Ravan Press, 1989.
41. Hlokoza Motau, interview, Johannesburg, 7 November 2011; Tshidi Mangoathe, interview, 18 May 2012.

42 Motau, interview, 7 November 2011. All Motau quotes in this chapter are from this interview.
43 Richard Stengel, *January Sun: One day, Three Lives, A South African Town,* New York: Simon & Schuster, 1990, p. 23.
44 *Brits Pos,* 10 April 1970.
45 Sello Selepe, interview, 26 April 2012. All Selepe quotes in this chapter are from this interview.
46 Banks, *Home Spaces, Street Styles,* 2011.
47 Stanley Uys, The Afrikaner establishment, in *No Turning Back,* edited by Shaun Johnson, London: Palgrave Macmillan, 1998.
48 Bert Botha, interview, 18 May 2012. All Botha quotes in this chapter are from this interview.
49 Ivor Chipkin, interview, 6 February 2012.
50 Alan Morris, The South African state and the Oukasie removal, *Transformation,* 8, 1989.
51 Sello Ramakobye, interview, 16 February 2012. All Ramakobye quotes in this chapter are from this interview.
52 Stengel, *January Sun,* p. 69.
53 Jacob Moatshe, interview, 5 November 2011. All Moatshe quotes in this chapter are from this interview.
54 Black Sash, *The Myth of Voluntary Removals.*
55 The removal process has been well documented. For a more detailed account of resistance and legal battles see: Morris, The South African State and the Oukasie Removal; S. Bekker, A. Morris, M. Orkin, M. Buys, G. Budlender, and A. Jeffrey, *Socio-economic Sample Survey of Oukasie,* Johannesburg: Community Agency for Social Enquiry, 1988; R. Abel, *Politics by Other Means,* New York: Routledge, 1995.
56 Richard Abel, *Politics by Other Means,* p. 286.
57 Caleb Dube, interview, 24 November 2011. All Dube quotes in this chapter are from this interview.
58 Stengel, *January Sun,* p. 122.
59 Stengel, *January Sun,* p. 91.
60 TRAC, Newsletter No. 11, July 1986, p. 4.
61 Simon Bekker et al., *Socio-economic Sample Survey of Oukasie,* p. 130.
62 Caroline Dikeledi Mashike, interview, 22 November 2011. All Mashike quotes in this chapter are from this interview.
63 Carole Cooper, Bantustan attitudes to trade unions, *South African Review 2,* Johannesburg: Ravan Press, 1984.
64 David Cooper, Ownership and control of commercial agriculture, *South African Review 4,* Johannesburg: Ravan Press, 1987.
65 Aninka Claasens, Rural land struggles in the Transvaal in the 1980s, *Umhlaba,* TRAC/Black Sash, November 1989.
66 Morris, The South African state and the Oukasie removal.
67 Tshidi Mangoathe, interview, 18 May 2012. All Mangoathe quotes in this chapter are from this interview.
68 TRAC, *Eastern District Land Reform Case Studies, Volume 4, Maboloka,* Johannesburg: TRAC, 1994, p. 4.
69 Stengel, *January Sun,* p. 41.

70 Tshidi Mangoathe, interview, 18 May 2012.
71 Black Sash, *The Myth of Voluntary Removals*.
72 TRAC, Newsletter No. 11, p. 4.
73 T. Mangoathe, N. Matlhare, S. Shozi, M. Mongoathe and D. Mathebula in consultation with E. Mayisela, S. Magakwe, S. Mkhabela, E.M. Matome and F. Mpete, The History of Brits Old Loction [sic], Oukasie, undated.
74 Amartya Sen, *The Idea of Justice,* London: Allen Lane, 2005, pp. 191 and 207.
75 Abel, *Politics by Other Means*, p. 495.
76 Abel, *Politics by Other Means*, p. 499.
77 Truth and Reconciliation Commission, Human Rights Violations 08-05-1997 David Modimoeng, http://www.justice.gov.za/trc/hrvtrans/mabopane/modim.htm.
78 http://www.justice.gov.za/trc/decisions%5C2001/ac21240.htm. Unless otherwise indicated, all information attributed to Pretorius is based on this source.
79 I was not able to interview Pretorius despite his willingness. Repeated requests from the Department of Justice for permission to interview Pretorius, who still worked in the Explosives Unit in Brits, were ignored.
80 Ac/2001/240 Truth and Reconciliation Commission: Amnesty Committee. Arson in respect of the bombing of houses belonging to David Modimeng [sic], to Leonard Brown and the murder of Joyce Modimeng [sic]. Paul Jacobus Jansen van Vuuren 1st applicant, Robert Leslie Jubber 2nd applicant, Machiel Andries Stephanus Pretorius 3rd applicant, Johannes Jacobus Victor (jnr) 4th applicant, Jan Hatting Cronje 5th applicant, Jacques Hechter 6th applicant. http://www.justice.gov.za/trc/decisions/2001/ac21240.htm. Hatting, Cronje, Jubber and Hechter were granted amnesty for conspiracy to murder Leonard Brown, Sello Ramakobye, David Modimoeng and Joyce Modimoeng in 1986. Pretorius stated that it was customary for Security Police members to intimidate activists by torching their houses or killing them.
81 Mangoathe et al., The History of Brits Old Loction.
82 Mangoathe et al., The History of Brits Old Loction.
83 Abel, *Politics by Other Means,* p. 502.
84 Alan Morris, Forced removals continue: Old Brits Location under threat, *South African Labour Bulletin,* Vol 2 No 8, 1986, p. 47.
85 Quoted in Stengel, *January Sun,* p. 123.
86 Abel, *Politics by Other Means,* p. 511.
87 Abel, *Politics by Other Means,* p. 515.

Chapter 3

88 Dumortier, *Pour ne pas Oublier,* p. 133.
89 Dumortier, Pour ne pas *Oublier,* p. 133.
90 Dumortier gave Brown and Molokoane the pseudonyms of Larry and Sam respectively, but all the people I interviewed named them openly.

91 Dumortier, *Pour ne pas Oublier,* p. 133.
92 Dumortier, *Pour ne pas Oublier,* p. 134.
93 Jacob Moatshe, interview, 5 November 2011. All Moatshe quotes in this chapter are from this interview.
94 Dumortier, *Pour ne pas Oublier,* p. 133.
95 Dumortier, *Pour ne pas Oublier,* p. 134.
96 Stengel, *January Sun*, p. 103.
97 Dumortier, *Pour ne pas Oublier* p. 134.
98 Sello Ramakobye, interview, 16 February 2012. All Ramakobye quotes in this chapter by are from this interview.
99 http://www.truthintranslation.org/educational_materials.pdf.
100 Sello Selepe, interview, 26 April 2012. All Selepe quotes in this chapter are from this interview.
101 A. Minnaar, I. Liebenberg and C. Schutte (eds.), *The Hidden Hand: Covert Operations in South Africa,* Pretoria: Human Sciences Research Council, 1994.
102 Truth and Reconciliation Amnesty Committee, http://www.justice.gov.za/trc/decisions/2001/ac21063.htm ac/2001/063. The murder squad then drove to a plot in Pretoria North where they hosed down the inside of the minibus "because Ngqulunga had urinated [during his assault] and so forth". The squad then drove to Pretoria where they had drinks and went to a restaurant.
103 Hlokoza Motau, interview, 7 November 2011. All Motau quotes in this chapter are from this interview. See Kally Forrest, *Metal that will not Bend,* for information about attacks on NUMSA trade unionists on the East Rand.
104 Peter Magagula, interview, 14 February 2012. All Magagula quotes in this chapter are from this interview.
105 Solly Phetoe, interview, 15 May 2012. All Phetoe quotations in this chapter are from this interview.
106 Dumortier, *Pour ne pas Oublier,* p. 138.
107 Dumortier, *Pour ne pas Oublier,* p. 139.
108 Tshidi Mangoathe, interview, 18 May 2012. All Mangoathe quotes in this chapter are from this interview.
109 In interviews people often mentioned being afraid of the Varksquad.
110 Stengel, *January Sun,* p. 126.
111 Stengel, *January Sun,* p. 126.
112 Jacob Moatshe recalls that Fankie Pretorius told him at the TRC, "You have so many spies in your midst and some are up there in Parliament."
113 *Sunday Nation*, 14 November 1993; Janine Rauch, Drive-by shootings in 1993, Seminar No. 9, 24 November 1993, presented at the Centre for the Study of Violence and Reconciliation, Johannesburg.
114 Bill Keller, Deadly free market: South Africa's warrior taxis, *New York Times,* 17 August 1993, http://www.nytimes.com/1993/08/17/world/deadly-free-market-south-africa-s-warrior-taxis.html?pagewanted=all&src=pm.
115 Jacob Moatshe and Sello Ramakobye, interviews.
116 Fana Peete, Tshwane's long-running taxi war ends, IOL News, 2

October 2006, http://www.iol.co.za/news/south-africa/tshwane-slong-running-taxi-war-ends-1.295829#.T-GierVBmSo.
117 Jerry Thibedi, speech made at opening of offices of Lethlabile-Brits United Local and Long Distance Taxi Association (Lebulldta), in Lethlabile, near Brits, Sunday, October 1, 2006.
118 This information is taken from testimony presented to the Truth and Reconciliation Commission. Ac/99/0221 Truth and Reconciliation Commission Amnesty Committee. Petrus Johannes Rudolph applicant (am 6329/97). Eugene Ney Terreblanche applicant (am7994 /97). http://www.justice.gov.za/trc/decisions/1999/ac990221.htm.
119 Japie Steenkamp, interview, 15 February 2012. All Steenkamp quotes in this chapter are from this interview.
120 Dumortier, *Pour ne pas Oublier,* p. 138.
121 Abel, *Politics by Other Means,* p. 521.
122 Janine Rauch, A preliminary assessment of the impact of the Peace Accord Code of Conduct on Police Behaviour, in *Policing in the New South Africa II,* Durban, August 1992, http://www.csvr.org.za/wits/papers/papeasjr.htm.
123 Antonio Gramsci, *Selections from the Prison Notebooks,* edited and translated by Quentin Hoare and Geoffrey Nowell, London: Lawrence and Wishart, 1971, p. 276.

Chapter 4

124 Dumortier, *Pour ne pas Oublier,* p. 143.
125 Sello Selepe, interview, 26 April 2012. All Selepe quotes in this chapter are from this interview.
126 Jacob Moatshe, interview, 5 November 2011. All Moatshe quotes in this chapter are from this interview.
127 Taffy Adler, interview, 7 December 2011. All Adler quotes in this chapter are from this interview.
128 Lynn Pikholz, Managing politics and storytelling: Meeting the challenge of upgrading informal housing in South Africa, *Habitat,* Vol 21, No 4, 1997, p. 377.
129 Caroline Mashike, interview, 22 November 2011. All Mashike quotes in this chapter are from this interview.
130 Japie Steenkamp, interview, 15 February 2012. All Steenkamp quotes in this chapter are from this interview.
131 Pikholz, *Managing Politics and Storytelling.*
132 Pikholz, *Managing Politics and Storytelling,* p. 383.
133 Pikholz, *Managing Politics and Storytelling,* p. 378.
134 Hlokoza Motau, interview, 7 November 2011. All Motau quotes in this chapter are from this interview.
135 Oukasie Development Trust, *Annual Report 1995.*
136 Oukasie Development Trust, *Annual Report 1995.*
137 Oukasie Development Trust, *Annual Report 1995.*
138 Oukasie Development Trust, *Annual Report 1996.*

139 Oukasie Development Trust, *Annual Report 1998*.
140 Oukasie Development Trust, *Annual Report 1998, 1999*.
141 Georgina Jaffee, Failure and success of the Thusanang co-operative, *South African Labour Bulletin,* Vol 13, No. 3, 1988.
142 Oukasie Development Trust, *Annual Report 1997, 1998, 1999*.
143 Jacob Moatshe and Tshidi Mangoathe.
144 Bert Botha, interview, 18 May 2012. All Botha quotes in this chapter are from this interview.
145 Bert Badenhorst, interview, 22 November 2011. All Badenhorst quotes in this chapter are from this interview.

Chapter 5

146 Transitional Local Council Brits Council Meeting, 25 May 1995.
147 Sello Selepe. interview, 26 April 2012. All Selepe quotes in this chapter are from this interview.
148 Jacob Moatshe, interview, 5 November 2011. All Moatshe quotes in this chapter are from this interview.
149 Ivor Chipkin, interview, 6 February 2012.
150 Chipkin, interview, 6 February 2012.
151 Japie Steenkamp, interview, 15 February 2012. All Steenkamp quotes in this chapter are from this interview.
152 Solly Phetoe, interview, 15 May 2012. All quotations from Phetoe in the chapter are from this interview.
153 Bert Badenhorst, interview, 22 November 2011. All Badenhorst quotes in this chapter are from this interview.
154 Caroline Mashike, interview, 22 November 2011. All Mashike quotes in this chapter are from this interview.
155 Transitional Local Council Brits Council Meetings, 26 February 1996, 27 July 1996, 29 July 1996, 16 September 2006.
156 Caroline Mashike, interview, 22 November 2011.
157 Madibeng Council employee, interviewed on condition of anonymity, 15 February 2012.
158 Brits Transitional Local Council Meetings, 27 June 1996, 2 December 1998.
159 Brits Transitional Local Council Meeting, 16 September 2006.
160 iphone.cogta.gov.za/subwebsites/masakhane/masakhaneintroduction.htm, 1 August 2012.
161 Brits Transitional Local Council Meeting, 19 April 1999.
162 In June 1998, for instance, the Council resolved to increase water, sewerage, refuse removal and household rates by 15%, by 21% for business and by 25% for industry. In May 1999 the cost of household water was increased by 18% and sewerage tariffs by 20% (Brits Transitional Local Council Meeting, 3 June 1998).
163 Sanlam equity worth R1 833 333 and Old Mutual policies worth R3 240 897 were traded in.
164 Brits Transitional Local Council Meeting, 14 December 1998: Cash

Flow Analysis of Council.
165 Brits Transitional Local Council Meetings, 15 January 1996, 13 May 1996, 27 July 1996.
166 Brits Transitional Local Council Meeting, 29 January 1996.
167 Brits Transitional Local Council Meeting, 22 February 1999.
168 Oukasie Development Trusts, *Annual Report*, 1996.
169 Peter Magagula, interview, 14 February 2012.
170 http://www.madibeng.gov.za/Madibeng_home_files/Madibeng_home_files/Annual%20Report%202005%20%202006%20VANTAGE%20Final%2021.08.2007.pdf 28/7/2012.
171 Madibeng council employee, interviewed on condition of anonymity, 15 February 2012.
172 It was a constant refrain in all interviews conducted.
173 Caleb Dube, interview, 24 November 2011. All Dube quotes in this chapter are from this interview.
174 Brits Transitional Local Council Meeting, 29 January 1996.
175 Brits Transitional Local Council Meeting, 22 February 1999.
176 Brits Transitional Local Council Meeting, 27 July 1998.
177 Brits Transitional Local Council Meeting, 19 April 1999.
178 Brits Transitional Local Council Meeting, 28 June 1999.
179 Ivor Chipkin, Set up for failure: Racial redress in the Department of Public Service Administration, in *Racial Redress & Citizenship*, edited by A. Habib and K. Bentley, Cape Town: HSRC Press, 2008.
180 Madibeng council employee, interviewed on condition of anonymity, 15 February 2012.
181 Jacob Modimoeng, interview, June 2011. All Modimoeng quotes in this chapter are from this interview.
182 This information was taken from a number of news reports at the time: IOL, http://www.iol.co.za/news/south-africa/fire-madibeng-mayorresidents-1.475755 27 July 2012; SAPA, 9 March 2010 at 02:58 pm; Classic FM, Brits municipal workers on strike, http://jeannine.classicfm.co.za/news/latest-news/brits-municipal-workers-on-strike; Brits march peaceful, 9 March 2010.
183 This information was taken from a number of news reports at the time: News 24, http://www.news24.com/SouthAfrica/News/Cops-fire-at-Brits-protesters-20100225, 11:44, 25 February 2010; News 24, http://www.news24.com/SouthAfrica/News/148-held-in-Brits-protest-20100303, 21:22, 3 March 2010.
184 Caleb Dube, interview, 24 November 2011; Brits taxi drivers protest over licences, News 24, 16:35, 9 November 2011.
185 Sello Ramakobye, interview, 16 February 2012. All Ramakobye quotes in this chapter are from this interview; Thabo Rantlha, Madibeng mayor ready to challenge Cosatu, *The New Age*, 26 September 2011, http://www.thenewage.co.za/Detail.aspx?news_id=30046&cat_id=1017.
186 Peter Magagula, interview, 14 February 2012.
187 *The Smoke that Calls,* Johannesburg: CSVR and SWOP, University of the Witwatersrand, 2011.

188 The average score of all municipalities was 48 (out of 100) in 2010. The lowest-scoring municipality was Madibeng (Brits) with 16 points, http://news.mobilitate.co.za/tag/ratings-afrika/ 2/2/2012.
189 Japie Steenkamp, interview, 15 February 2012.
190 Hlokoza Motau, interview, 7 November 2011.
191 Amartya Sen, *The Idea of Justice*, pp. 85–86.
192 Catteeuw and Dumortier, *The Long Struggle Record of the YCWs of Africa*, pp. 95–96.

Chapter 6

193 *Kormorant*, 27 November 2015, 29 November 2017; https://www.iol.co.za/news/south-africa/north-west/cash-strapped-madibengmunicipality-denies-mayors-trip-to-cost-r1m-13031870.
194 https://www.pressreader.com/south-africa/sowetan/20180416/281651075694085.
195 https://kormorant.co.za/30732/madibeng-officials-overeat-whileresidents-sleep-on-an-empty-stomach.
196 https://www.iol.co.za/news/politics/national-government-takescontrol-of-north-west-report-14949944; http://ewn.co.za/2018/05/14/ramaphosa-to-meet-nw-anc-mahumapelo-over-govt-intervention.
197 https://www.iol.co.za/news/politics/madibeng-graft-officials-to-loseproperties-1646633.
198 Taffy Adler, interview, 7 December 2011.
199 Hlokoza Motau, interview, 7 November 2011.
200 Jean-Marie Dumortier, Obituary for David Modimoeng, South African YCW leader and trade union "prophet", http://saycwstruggle.blogspot.com/2009/01/background-to-initiative.html, 2009.
201 Solly Phetoe, interview, 15 May 2012.
202 Bert Badenhorst, interview, 22 November 2011.

Bibliography

Abel, Richard. *Politics by Other Means.* New York: Routledge, 1995.

Banks, Leslie J. *Home Spaces, Street Styles: Contesting Power and Identity in a South African City.* London and Johannesburg: Pluto Press and Wits University Press, 2011.

Bekker, Simon, Alan Morris, Mark Orkin, Marshall Buys, Geoff Budlender, and Anthea Jeffrey. *Socio-economic Sample Survey of Oukasie.* Johannesburg: Community Agency for Social Enquiry, 1988.

Black Sash. *The Myth of Voluntary Removals.* Johannesburg: Black Sash, undated.

Brits Town Council. *Gedenk Album Brits 1924–1974.* Brits: Town Council, 1974.

Catteeuw, Karl and Jos Dumortier (eds.). *The Long Struggle Record of the YCWs of Africa. 75th Anniversary of the Young Christian Workers.* Brussels: International Cardijn Foundation, 2000.

Centre for the Study of Violence and Reconciliation (CSVR) and Society, Work and Development Institute (SWOP) (eds.). *The Smoke That Calls.* Johannesburg: CSVR and SWOP, University of the Witwatersrand, 2011.

Claasens, Aninka. Rural land struggles in the Transvaal in the 1980s. *Umhlaba,* November 1989.

Cooper, Carole. Bantustan attitudes to trade unions. *South African Review 2,* edited by South African Research Service. Johannesburg: Ravan Press, 1984.

Cooper, David. Ownership and control of commercial agriculture. *South African Review 4.* Johannesburg: Ravan Press, 1987.

Dumortier, Jean-Marie. *Pour ne pas vous oublier: Prêtre en Afrique du sud.* Editions ouvrières (French edition), 1991.

Dumortier, Jean-Marie. Obituary for David Modimoeng, South African YCW leader and trade union "prophet". http://saycwstruggle.

blogspot.com/2009/01/background-to-initiative.html, 2009.

Forrest, Kally. *Metal That Will Not Bend: National Union of Metal Workers of South Africa 1980–1995.* Johannesburg: Wits University Press, 2011.

Gramsci, Antonio. *Selections from the Prison Notebooks,* edited and translated by Quentin Hoare and Geoffrey Nowell. London: Lawrence and Wishart, 1971.

Habib, Adam and Kristina Bentley (eds.). *Racial Redress and Citizenship.* Cape Town: HSRC Press, 2008.

International Young Christian Workers (IYCW). *Declaration of Principles.* sources.cardijncommunityaustralia.org/the, 1975, (accessed 12 March 2012).

Jaffee, Georgina. Living with unemployment: Strategies for survival. *Work in Progress,* 34: 16, October 1984.

Johnson, Shaun. *No Turning Back.* London: Palgrave Macmillan, 1998.

Keenan, Jeremy. The B&S closure: Rationalisation or reprisal? *South African Labour Bulletin,* 10(1): 77, 1984.

Keller, Bill. Deadly free market: South Africa's warrior taxis. *New York Times,* 17 August 1993. http://www.nytimes.com/1993/08/17/world/deadly-free-market-south-africa-s-warrior-taxis.html?pagewanted=all&src=pm.

Lowry, Donovan. *20 Years in the Labour Movement.* Johannesburg: Wadmore Publishing, 1999.

Mangoathe, T., N. Matlhare, S. Shozi, M. Mongoathe and D. Mathebula in consultation with E. Mayisela, S. Magakwe, S. Mkhabela, E.M. Matome and F. Mpete. The History of Brits Old Loction [sic], Oukasie, unpublished manuscript, undated.

Minnaar, Anthony, Ian Liebenberg and Charl Schutte (eds.). *The Hidden Hand: Covert Operations in South Africa.* Pretoria: Human Sciences Research Council, 1994.

Morris, Alan. Forced removals continue: Old Brits Location under threat. *South African Labour Bulletin,* 2(8): 47, 1986.

Morris, Alan. The South African state and the Oukasie removal. *Transformation,* 8: 24–46, 1989.

Newton, Deborah. Forced removals in South Africa. *South African Review 5,* edited by South African Research Service. Johannesburg: Ravan Press, 1989.

Peete, Fana. Tshwane's long-running taxi war ends. IOL News, 2 October 2006. http://www.iol.co.za/news/south-africa/tshwane-s-longrunning-taxi-war-ends-1.295829#.T-GierVBmSo.

Platzky, Laurine. Reprieves and repression: Relocation in South Africa. *South African Review 3,* edited by South African Research Service. Johannesburg: Ravan Press, 1986.

Rauch, Janine. A Preliminary Assessment of the Impact of the Peace Accord Code of Conduct on Police Behaviour. Paper presented at the Policing in the New South Africa II Conference, Centre for Criminal Justice, Durban, August 1992.

Sen, Amartya. *The Idea of Justice.* London: Allen Lane, 2005.

Stengel, Richard. *January Sun: One Day, Three Lives, A South African Town.* New York: Simon & Schuster, 1990.

Transvaal Rural Action Committee (TRAC). The Old Brits Location (Oukasie): A clear indication that forced removals have not stopped. *TRAC Newsletter,* No. 11, July 1986. Johannesburg: Black Sash.

Transvaal Rural Action Committee (TRAC). *Eastern District Land Reform Case Studies, Volume 4, Maboloka.* Johannesburg: Black Sash, 1994.

Truth and Reconciliation Commission (TRC). Human Rights Violations 08-05-1997 David Modimoeng. http://www.justice.gov.za/trc/hrvtrans/mabopane/modim.htm, 1997.

Uys, Stanley. The Afrikaner establishment. In *No Turning Back*, edited by S. Johnson. London: Palgrave Macmillan, 1998.

Interviews

Adler, Taffy – former organiser of the National Automobile and Allied Workers' Union and vice-chairperson of the Oukasie Development Trust, interviewed 7 December 2011

Badenhorst, Bert – former head of human resources at Robert Bosch, and member of the Brits Industrial Association, which was later known as the Madibeng Business Forum, interviewed 22 November 2011

Botha, Bert – Conservative Party mayor of Brits and dentist in Hartbeespoort Dam, interviewed 18 May 2012

Chipkin, Ivor – former Director of the Public Affairs Research Institute, interviewed 6 February 2012

Cloete, Moses – general secretary of the YCW in South Africa and later its international secretary, interviewed 25 October 2011

Dantjies, Peter – early Brits YCW member, dismissed Femco worker, B&S organiser, National Union of Metalworkers of South Africa organiser, assistant general secretary and Northern Transvaal regional secretary, interviewed June 1997

Dube, Caleb – former Afrox worker, member of the Brits Action Committee and Steel Engineering and Allied Workers' Union of South Africa before promotion to production foreman, resident of Lethlabile, interviewed 24 November 2011

Magagula, Peter – former Firestone head shop steward in Brits, residing in Lethlabile, interviewed 14 February 2012

Mangoathe, Tshidi – early Brits YCW and Metal and Allied Workers Union member, a Madibeng councillor and later Madibeng mayor, interviewed 18 May 2012

Mashike, Caroline Dikeledi – school principal, ODT Trustee and Madibeng councillor, interviewed 22 November 2011

Moatshe, Jacob – teacher and early Brits YCW member, ODT Community Liaison Officer, ODT Chief Executive Officer, interviewed 5 November 2011

Modimoeng, Jacob – brother to David Modimoeng, Brits YCW member, and provincial secretary of the South African Municipal Workers Union in the North West

Motau, Hlokoza – Brits YCW member and organiser, international officer of the National Union of Metalworkers of South Africa, interviewed 7 November 2011

Phetoe, Solly – former organiser for the National Union of Metalworkers of South Africa, organiser and North West regional secretary for the Congress of South African Trade Unions, interviewed 15 May 2012

Ramakobye, Sello – Brits YCW member and former Firestone head shop steward in Brits who moved to Firestone's Port Elizabeth branch, now retired in Oukasie, interviewed 16 February 2012

Selepe, Sello – Oukasie resident, North West provincial chairperson of the South African Municipal Workers' Union, interviewed 26 April 2012

Steenkamp, Japie – Brits National Party councillor between 1970 and 1990, owner of Brits Print and ODT Trustee, interviewed 15 February 2012

Index

f) following a number indicates that the reference is to a footnote on that page.

Numbers in *italics* indicate photographs.

Aap, Arnold 91
accountability, ethics of viii
Adler, Taffy 144–5
    B&S strike 13, 14
    Brits Action Committee 52
    Oukasie Development Trust 89,
        91–2, 96, 101, 111
African Christian Democratic Party
    (ACDP) 110
African National Congress (ANC)
    20, 105–111, 112
African Telephone Cables 123
Afrikaner Weerstandsbeweging
    (AWB) 82–3, 106–7, 109
Afrox 18, 37
Alexandra Action Committee 53, 77
Alfa Romeo 3, 18, 39
askaris 60, 60(f), 72–5, 81
Auto Cables 18, 44, 50
Autocast 50, 118, 123

B&S strike 12–20
Badenhorst, Bert 98, 108–110,
    118–19, 121, 123, 146
Bakwena FC 42
Bakwena ba Magopa 40

Bam, Brigalia 68(f)
Bantustans 2, 23, 29, 123
Bapong 106, 139
Barayi, Elijah 60
Barnard, Otto 92
Battle of Ventersdorp 83
Bellingham (Captain) 73
Black Sash 22(f), 34, 47, 50, 52, 53,
    63, 90, 92
Bleibaum, Ulli 92, 93–4
Bokfontein 73
Bophuthatswana 3, 12, 23, 24, 39–41
Bophuthatswana Radio 17, 41
Borders of Particular States
    Extension Act (1980) 23
Botha, Bert (Dr) 28, 29, 107, 108, 110
Botha, P.W. 28
Botlhabelo High School 47
Bouwer Viljoen (Engineers) 92
Braklaagte 40
Brits
    early history 1–4
    swing to the right 27–32
    See also Madibeng Municipality
Brits Action Committee (BAC) 20,
    33–4, 42, 45–7, 50, 51, 61–2, 89

Brits Coordinating Committee 109, 110
Brits Industrial Association 54, 118
Brits Long Distance Taxi Association 81
Brits Morning Stars FC 42
Brits Rate Payers Association 112
Brits Sakekamer 109
Brits Transitional Council *See* Transitional Local Council (Brits)
Brits Youth Committee 76
Brown, Leonard 55, 57–9, 68–70, 75, 78, 81, 107
Brown, Marj 52
Budlender, Geoff 52, 54, 91, 96, 100
Buys, Marshall 19, *70*
   Brits Action Committee 34, 46, 52, 71, 77
   violence in Oukasie 55, 69–70, 75, 76, 78–9

Cardijn, Joseph 4
Central Transvaal Development Board 54
Chaskalson, Arthur 52, 65, 65(f)
Christian Institute of Southern Africa 60
Claasens, Aninka 52
Cloete, Moses 6, 9
Congress of South African Students (COSAS) 20, 138
Congress of South African Trade Unions (COSATU) 60, 109, 130, 143
Conservative Party (in Brits) 27–8, 54, 65, 66, 83, 95, 107–110
Convention for a Democratic South Africa (CODESA), 108(f)
Corians FC 42
Covenant Programme 51–2
Cronje, Jack (Brigadier) 57
Cruywagen, Willem 65

Damonsville 75, 86, 134
Daniel, George F. (Bishop) 8, 34
Dantjies, Peter 11–13, 18, 19, 143
De Beer, M.B. 54

deconcentration area 2
Defence of the Rights of Man 71
De Jager, Nicholas 109–110
De Klerk, F.W. 83
Demarcation Board 125
Democratic Alliance (DA) 134
Democratic Party (DP) 110
Department of Land Affairs 122
Dube, Caleb 33, 35–7, 53, 134, 145–6
Dumortier, Jean-Marie 3, 17, 51, 146
   developing Oukasie 88–9, 92
   discipline 60–1, 145
   role of churches 84
   trade union formation 19
   violence in Oukasie 67–71
Duncan, Sheena 52

Elandsrand 25, 134
Evaton 43, 44

Fafung 43
Fanaroff, Bernie 52
Federated Chamber of Industry (FCI) 54
Federation of South African Trade Unions (FOSATU) 12, 46, 142
Femco 11
Firestone 3, 18, *19*, 50–1, 118
forced removals
   nature of 22–3, 26–7, 32
   resistance to 32–65
   role of women 50
Friends of Oukasie *See* Oukasie People's Delegation

Ga-Rankuwa 23, 40, 41, 123, 139
Genuine Representation Campaign 10–11
Gerber, Andrew 65
gerrymandering 45, 45(f)
governance, accountable vii–ix
Greater Brits Development Forum 105, 117–18
Greater Brits Investment Group (GBIG) 105–6
Group Areas Act (1950) 44
Gundle Industries 17

Habitat for Humanity 103
Hanekom, Derek 100
Hani, Chris 74, 74(f), 86
Happy Hearts FC 34, 42
Hartebeesfontein 24, 72
Hechter, Jacques (Lt) 57, 59–60
Herstigte Nasionale Party (HNP) 28, 110
Hertzog, J.B.M. (General) 2
Heunis, J.C. (Chris) 51, 54, 62, 63, 64–5
Hlongwane, Jane 36
Hlongwane, Uniboy 52, 52(f)
Holicki, Otto 93–4, 96
homelands *See* Bantustans
Hough, Danie 84–5
Hurley, Denis (Archbishop) 4

Independent Development Trust (IDT) 91, 92, 105
Industrial Conciliation Act (Bop, 1983) 39
industrial decentralised zones 23
Integrated Development Plan 134
Internal Security Act (Bop, 1979) 39
Itumeleng Primary School 63

Jericho 43, 80, 121, 139
Joint Parents Committee 48, 49
Justice and Peace Commission 34
Jubber, Robert (Capt.) 57, 76, 78–9

Kagiso Trust 98
Khoza, Ellen *17*, 48, 50, 145
Khoza, July 19, 113, 143
Khumalo, Sam 32–3
Koevoet 41(f), 74
Kompe, Lydia 52, 53
Kopano, Lawrence 81–2
Kruger, James T. 7
KwaNdebele 40

Labour Relations Act (1995) 125
Land Administration Act (1995) 101
leadership
    importance of viii, 96, 97, 132–5, 137
    nature of 141–2

Legal Resources Centre (LRC) 52
Lethlabile
    askaris 72–5
    Concerned Citizens 132
    development of 32, 86
    service delivery 124–5, 131–2
    type of township 20, 24, 27, 37
    taxi violence 80–2
Lethlabile-Brits United Local and Long Distance Taxi Association (Lebulldta) 81
Lethlabile Taxi Association (LTA) 81
Local Government Demarcation Boards 108
Local Government Transition Act (1993) 101, 108
Local Government Transitional Amendment Act (1996) 112
Lodger's Permit Committee 47

Maboloka 32, 45, 80, 106, 121, 139
Mabopane 23
Madibeng Municipality (incorporating Brits and Oukasie) 42, 113, 116
    corruption 126–31
    finances 121–23
    service delivery 123–26, 132, 134, 137, 139–42
    See also Brits, Lethlabile, Oukasie
Madumo, David 48, 145
Magagula, Peter 19, 74, 75, 85, 86, 125, 133, 135
Magakwe, Jacob "Commodore" 51
Mahlaela, Moshe 53–4, 145
Majakaneng 106
Makama, Joseph 65
Makgale, Wanda 50, 107, 145
Makhura, Pat 41
Mamabolo, Levy *93*, 107, 109, 145
    anti-removal activities 48
    B&S strike 18
    leadership 19, 118
    Oukasie Development Trust 94, 100–1
    Transitional Local Council 113–16, 123, 125
Mamasela, Joe 60, 72

Mamelodi 81
Mandela, Nelson 88, 106–7, 121, 135–6, *136*
Mangena, Mike 81–2
Mangoathe, Malasba Lazarus 35, *36*
Mangoathe, Tshidi 19, 42–4, 50, 53, 76, 107, 113, *144*
Mangope, Lucas 41
Marais, Jaap 28
Masakhane Project 121–2
Mashike, Caroline 37, 64, 94, 104, 107, 113, 120, 145
Masithela, Nana 130
Matatiele 50
Matlhare, Nankie 48, 50, 145–6
Mayekiso, Moses 77
Mayisela, Eliot 95, 106
Mdaka, Moses 81–2
Metal and Allied Workers Union (MAWU) 4, 13–14, 18, 44, 63
Mkhabela, Sam 105, 113
Mkhatshwa, Smangaliso (Father) 34, 71, 71(f)
Mmakau 40
Mmokobyane (General) 41
Moatshe, Jacob, *93*, 144
   activities in Bop 40, 41
   anti-removal activities 42–4, 47, 53, 60–1
   Oukasie Development Trust 89, 94, 96–7, 101, 104, 105, 111
   removals to Lethlabile 33, 51
   Transitional Local Council 113–14, 117–18
   violence in Oukasie 55, 69, 72(f), 74, 76, 84
   YCW training 6–7, 10
Moatshe, Peter 95
Modimoeng, David 11–13, 19, 55–6, *58*, 59–60, 63, 116–17, 145
Modimoeng, Jacob 130, 146
Modimoeng, Joyce 59–61, *61*
Mokase, David 113
Mokhari, Annah 48
Molefe, Brian 147(f)
Molefe, Popo 69, 84
Molokoane, Abel 74–5, 89
Molokoane, Rose 102

Molokoane-Machika, Sophie 131
Monare, Blacky 62
Mongalo, Chippa 34, 42, 89
Moosa, Valli 117
Mopedi, George 33
Morris, Alan 52, 63
Morulane, Jerry 107
Motau, Hlokoza 23–4, 51, 143, 145
   developing Oukasie 98
   leadership 19, 133
   Robert Bosch strike 49
   taxi violence 80
   township permit system 47
   violence in Oukasie 73, 75, 79
   YCW training 8, 10
Mothibe, Jostine 140
Mothutlung 3, 23, 24 41, 86, 106
Motsepe, Raymond 118
Moutse 50, 53
Mpete, Mary 62
Municipal Finance Management Act (2003) 120

National African Federated Chamber of Commerce and Industry (NAFCOC) 118
National Automobile and Allied Workers' Union (NAAWU) 13, 18, 63
National Education Coordinating Council (NECC) 79
National Housing Commission 99, 101–2
National Party
   Brits 65, 66, 83, 108, 110, 112
   nationally 2, 29–30
National Peace Accord 85, 86
National Union of Mineworkers (NUM) 143
National Union of Metalworkers of South Africa (NUMSA) 8, 109, 123, 142–3
Naude, Beyers 60
necklacing 78(f)
New Public Management (NPM) (model) 127
Ngale, Phineas 89, 95, 107, 145, 147(f)
Ngqulunga, Brian 73

Nofomela, Almond 73
Northern Transvaal Chamber of Commerce 54
North West Business Forum 118

Oelofse, Michael 92
Ossewabrandwag 2
Oukasie
   destroying resistance 67–71
   development of 90–105, 123
   disestablishment 62–5
   early history 1, 2–4, 24–5,
   feasibility study 63
   reasons for removal 25–7
   reasons for resistance 38–45
   resistance to removal 21–65
   service delivery 115, 131–2, 140
   taxi violence 80–2
   violent backlash 66–87
   See also Madibeng Municipality
Oukasie Civic Association (OCA) 89, 95
Oukasie Development Trust (ODT) viii, 88–111, 124
Oukasie People's Delegation 89, 91
Oukasie Residents Committee 67–68
Oukasie Women's Movement 50

Phakoe, Moss 147
Phasha, Cyprian 107
Phetoe, Solly 74, 146, 147(f)
Platinum Development Trust 144
Pretorius, Machiel (Fankie) 56, 57–60, 78
Prevention of Illegal Squatting Act (1951) 65
Primindia 106
Progressive Federal Party (PFP) 28

Radio Bop *See* Bophuthatswana Radio
Ramakobye, Sello 19, 37, *48*, 143, 145, 146
   apartheid reprisals 55, 57–9
   Brits Action Committee 46
   community organisation 132–3
   violence in Oukasie 77

Reconstruction and Development Programme (RDP) 116
Ramaphosa, Cyril 60, 141
Ratlou, A.D. 118
Regional Services Council 99
removals *See* forced removals
Robert Bosch 3, 18, 49
Rosslyn 123

Sectoral Determination for Farm Workers 125
Segwaelane 106
Selepe, Sello 25–6, 47, 49, 107, 143
   development of Oukasie 89, 90
   leadership 134
   service delivery 128
   Transitional Local Council 113, 116, 117, 122
   violence in Oukasie 72, 76–7, 79, 84
Sexwale, Tokyo 86
Shiceka, Sicelo 130, 147
Skeerpoort 73
Soshanguve 24, 139
South African Communist Party (SACP) 6, 107, 130, 138
South African Congress of Trade Unions (SACTU) 46
South African Council of Churches (SACC) 51–2, 68, 68(f), 84
South African Development Trust 123
South African Federation of Trade Unions (SAFTU) 143
South African Homeless People's Federation 102–3
South African Municipal Workers' Union (SAMWU) 128–31, 134, 140, 143
South African National Civic Organisation (SANCO) 109, 130
South African National Student Congress (SANSCO) 79
Special Branch (South African Security Police) 57, 62
State of Emergency 52, 52(f), 56, 61, 77, 88, 113
Steel and Engineering Industries Federation of South Africa

(SEIFSA) 54
Steenkamp, Japie 21, 44, 83, 94–5, 97, 98, 108, 109, 110, 116, 119–20, 121, 124
Suzman, Helen 65

taxi violence 80–2
Tele, Johanna 62
Terreblanche, Eugene 83
Terrorism Act (1967) 7, 52(f)
Thibedi, Jerry 82
Tjale, Mack 33
township permit system 47
Trade Union Council of South Africa (TUCSA) 6
Transitional Local Council (TLC) (Brits) 100, 104, 110, 112, 121–3
See also Madibeng Municipality
Transvaal Provincial Authority (TPA) 64, 91, 92, 97
Transvaal Rural Action Committee (TRAC) 22, 34, 40, 44, 49, 50, 52, 53, 63
Treurnicht, Andries 27–8
Tricameral Parliament 29
Truth and Reconciliation Commission (TRC) 55
Tyacke, Eric 5–6, 8
Tyacke, Jean 6, 8

Umkhonto we Sizwe (MK) 20, 72
United Democratic Front (UDF) 6, 20, 46, 71, 72, 77, 89, 138
Urban Foundation 92
USAID 98

Van Dijkhorst, Kees (Justice) 65
Van Leer 123
Van Vuuren, Jacobus 60
Varksquad 75–80
Ventersdorp 40, 53, 83
Vereeniging 43
violence 132
  in Oukasie 55, 67–73, 75–9, 84
  taxi violence 80–2
Vlakplaas 73
Vorster, B.J. 2, 3
Vuka Swallows FC 42

Wolmarans, Matthew J. 147(f)
workerism vs populism 46(f)

Yawitch, Joanne 52
Young Christian Workers (YCW) viii, 137, 138–9, 142, 146
  IX World Council 135–6, 136
  early years in Oukasie 8–14
  formation 3, 4–6
  developing Oukasie 90–111
  super group 13
  training methods 3–4, 8–10
  working with trade unions 10–14
Young Worker (newspaper) 9, 10